Inductive Reasoning Tests

www.How2Become.com

As part of this product you have also received FREE access to online tests that will help you to pass Inductive Reasoning assessments

To gain access, simply go to:

www.MyPsychometricTests.co.uk

Get more products for passing any test at:

www.How2Become.com

Orders: Please contact How2Become Ltd, Suite 14, 50 Churchill Square Business Centre, Kings Hill, Kent ME19 4YU.

You can order through Amazon.co.uk under ISBN: 9781910602126, via the website www.How2Become.com or through Gardners.com.

ISBN: 9781910602126

First published in 2015 by How2Become Ltd.

Updated in 2018.

Typeset by Katie Noakes for How2Become Ltd.

Disclaimer

Every effort has been made to ensure that the information contained within this guide is accurate at the time of publication. How2Become Ltd is not responsible for anyone failing any part of any selection process as a result of the information contained within this guide. How2Become Ltd and their authors cannot accept any responsibility for any errors or omissions within this guide, however caused. No responsibility for loss or damage occasioned by any person acting, or refraining from action, as a result of the material in this publication can be accepted by How2Become Ltd.

The information within this guide does not represent the views of any third party service or organisation.

CONTENTS

INTRODUCTION

INTRODUCTION TO YOUR NEW GUIDE

Welcome to your new guide, Inductive Reasoning tests. This guide is a comprehensive testing book which provides plenty of practice questions for you to work through.

This book is aimed at anyone who wishes to successfully pass their Inductive Reasoning test. If you are asked to take an Inductive Reasoning test, you need to be able to complete the test with the best marks possible, and that is why we have created this guide in order to provide an understanding of what you can expect from your Inductive Reasoning assessment.

The key to success for psychometric testing books is practice and preparation. Try your hardest to get 100% in your answers; aiming for 100% will enable you to achieve success far more likely than if you sit a test in a negative frame of mind.

We have purposely provided you with lots of questions in order for you to gain a complete understanding of what you are likely to face in an Inductive Reasoning test.

It is important that when working through this book, you check your answers at the end of each testing chapter. Knowing where you went wrong and understanding what you need to do to reach the correct answer, is just as important as getting the correct answer. If you know how to fix your mistakes, you are far more likely to get the answer correct next time.

Good luck and we wish you all the best.

STRUCTURE OF THE BOOK

This book follows a very clear and simple structure in order for you to make the most out of your Inductive Reasoning testing guide.

We have provided you with six testing sections, each with a variety of questions and levels of difficulty for you to work through. Work through each chapter and then check your answers with the explanations provided.

This comprehensive Inductive Reasoning testing guide follows the structure as formulated below:

- Introduction – introducing your new guide
- About Inductive Reasoning tests
  - Who takes an Inductive Reasoning test
  - What is Inductive Reasoning?
  - What the questions look like
- Example Inductive Reasoning tests and how to answer them
- Inductive Reasoning Tests, Section 1
- Inductive Reasoning Tests, Section 2
- Inductive Reasoning Tests, Section 3
- Inductive Reasoning Tests, Section 4
- Inductive Reasoning Tests, Section 5
- Inductive Reasoning Tests, Section 6
- A Few Final Words...

ABOUT INDUCTIVE REASONING

WHO TAKES AN INDUCTIVE REASONING TEST?

An Inductive Reasoning test is often used in job selection processes to determine whether or not you are suitable for the job role. Inductive Reasoning has become a popular screening process, used by many employers to provide them with valuable information in regards to the way people think or react.

This test solely measures your ability to solve problems. These tests are designed to measure logical reasoning and perpetual reasoning skills. The skills you need to demonstrate in an Inductive Reasoning test are transferable skills that are applicable to most job roles, specifically to jobs involving engineering, science, IT or software development.

You may be required to sit an Inductive Reasoning test as an early screening process to eliminate candidates. You may also be required to sit the test alongside or before an interview, or you may be asked to take the test during an assessment day at an assessment centre.

As well as the Inductive Reasoning test, many selection processes also involve a Verbal and Non-Verbal test; therefore, it is important that you know how to successfully pass this stage of the selection process. Employers like to see candidates who show acute awareness and understanding of logical thinking and reasoning ability.

WHAT ARE INDUCTIVE REASONING TESTS?

Inductive Reasoning tests are similar to 'Diagrammatic' or 'Abstract' Reasoning tests, whereby the test requires you to identify patterns or consistencies amongst sets of objects, shapes or words.

These tests are often used interchangeably. While they are slightly different, the concept behind Inductive Reasoning and Abstract Reasoning remains the same. Both tests are used to assess a person's logical and problem solving skills.

It is common for Inductive Reasoning tests to present matrices of shapes and objects to highlight patterns and similarities, in order to illustrate what is happening as a sequence progresses. These tests are a form of aptitude assessment, which generates logical and methodical understanding.

It is often said that people who perform to a high standard in these tests, tend to have higher levels of capacity in regards to thinking conceptually and analytically; they draw upon patterns and configurations, something employers often admire.

WHAT TO EXPECT?

Inductive Reasoning tests provide a series of diagrams, of which there will be an underlying rule affecting the layout. Your job is to identify what is happening in the diagrams to determine the pattern of the sequence.

Typically, in an Inductive Reasoning test you will need to choose between 4-6 possible answers. It is important that you understand the pattern of the sequence before choosing your answer. The answers will all look very similar; and at first glance, may seem like the correct answer. However, if you have not distinguished the correct pattern or rule that is recurring, the chances are you will not choose the correct answer.

There is often a strict time limit for these tests and therefore many candidates find it difficult to complete the test within the given timeframe. We cannot stress enough that these tests are merely used to decipher whether or not you are suitable for the specific job role you're applying for. Therefore, employers are not looking for you to complete the test; moreover, they are looking at your accurate results, as well as efficiency.

AIMS FOR INDUCTIVE REASONING

For psychometric testing, you need to aim for speed as well as accuracy. It is important to be able to undergo these tests with the utmost confidence and composure, in order to work swiftly and effectively.

The aim of this book is simple; we want to ensure that you are provided with the best preparation and guidance when it comes to your Inductive Reasoning test. We take pride in helping others successfully pass psychometric tests and are proud to help people become one step closer to their goals and ambitions.

The main objective for us at How2become is to ensure that you are 100% comfortable with completing an Inductive Reasoning test; and to provide valuable and insightful knowledge and guidance in terms of Inductive Reasoning.

HOW CAN I PREPARE FOR AN INDUCTIVE REASONING TEST?

The only way to prepare for an Inductive Reasoning test, or any other form of psychometric testing, is simply through practising.

Practice is the best form of preparation. Most psychometric tests require you to be familiar with the concept and layout of the test in order to stand a chance of successfully passing. Practising will no doubt maximise your potential and performance and thus, increase your chances of success.

In order to succeed, you need to have a clear understanding of the principles and purpose of the test. You need to know what to expect and how to complete the questions, so it doesn't startle you on the day of your real test.

Practising beforehand will also give you some indication of how well you will perform these tests under severe time constraints. As mentioned earlier, the tests can be set under strict time limits; thus practising will not only enable you to determine how well you perform under these time limits, but also will help to improve your logical ability and timing skills.

Although we have provided you with lots of practice questions, depending on the type of test you are going to be taking, will depend on the types of questions you will have to answer. We have provided you with the main question types for any Inductive Reasoning test, which primarily focuses on your ability to identify sequences and patterns amongst shapes, objects or numbers.

WHAT DO THE QUESTIONS LOOK LIKE?

The types of questions that you will face in the Inductive Reasoning test will vary depending on the type of test you are sitting. However, this book provides you with a variety of sample questions and explanations in hope to give you a clear understanding of what to expect.

Inductive Reasoning is similar to tests like Abstract Reasoning; whereby it assesses a candidate's ability to visualise and identify patterned sequences. All the questions in this book are the types of questions you are likely to face. Each question is very similar, however, they do test different things; and it is important that you can identify what pattern is happening.

Inductive Reasoning includes questions regarding:

- Rotations

- Reflections

- Alternations

- Translations

- Replacements

- 3D shapes

This book provides an insight into Inductive Reasoning and hopes to assist you through the learning process. We have done our utmost to ensure that a range of testing questions are used throughout the book, allowing you to utilise your skills and knowledge in regards to Inductive Reasoning.

Before you begin the testing sections, you may wish to look through the next chapter, which gives clear examples of the types of questions you can expect to answer throughout the book. These example questions will provide a clear and detailed explanation of how to reach the answer, the process involved and what to look out for.

Finally, we have also provided you with some additional free online psychometric tests which will help to further improve your competence in this particular testing area.

To gain access, simply go to:

www.PsychometricTestsOnline.co.uk

Good luck and best wishes,

The how2become team

The How2Become Team

EXAMPLES FOR
INDUCTIVE REASONING

QUESTION TYPE I

Fill in the missing square in order to complete the sequence.

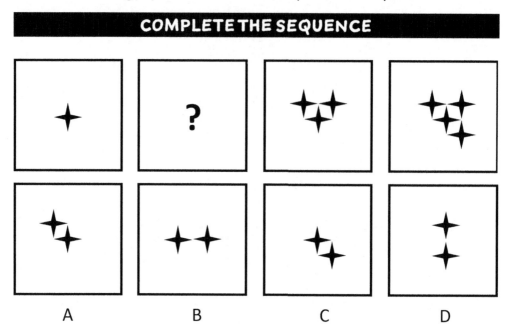

COMPLETE THE SEQUENCE

A   B   C   D

Answer = A

Rule 1 = the sequence adds one diamond each time. The diamond is added from the top left and then continues to be added in a clockwise manner.

For these types of questions, you need to pay particular attention to numbers. The sequence follows the pattern of adding the same shape as the sequence progresses.

In other similar questions, you may need to add or subtract certain numbers of shapes in order for the sequence to make sense.

QUESTION TYPE 2

Rotating the figures.

ROTATING THE FIGURES

A   B   C   D

Answer = D

Rule 1 = the cross moves one place clockwise.

Rule 2 = the grey dot moves one place clockwise.

Rule 3 = you will also notice that the sequence alternates its colours. The big shapes change from black to white. The cross changes from white to black. The dot remains the same colour.

For these types of questions, you need to understand what direction the sequence has been rotated. Not all the shapes will be rotated in the same direction, so pay attention to what is happening.

Also, you will have noticed that two different things are happening; rotation and alternation. Some questions may require you to identify more than one thing happening in the sequence.

Remember, if you struggle to find the pattern of a sequence, break it down! Take one shape at a time and determine what is happening to that shape as the sequence progresses. Do the same for all the shapes until you understand everything going on in the patterned sequence.

QUESTION TYPE 3

Which of the answer figures completes the sequence?

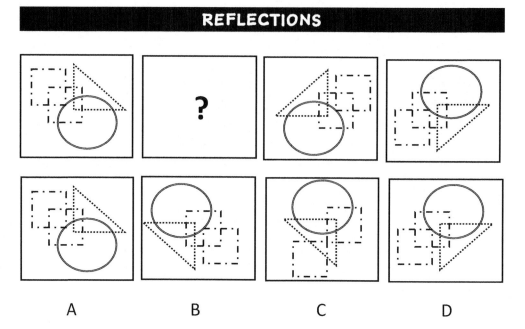

REFLECTIONS

A   B   C   D

Answer = B

Rule 1 = Box 1 and 3 are reflections of one another.

Rule 2 = Box 2 and 4 will be reflections of one another.

For these types of questions, you need to pay attention to what is being reflected.

The reflections may not be seen one after another; they may be reflecting every other box, or every third box, therefore it is important to look closely at everything that is going on and identify the pattern and similarities of each figure.

QUESTION TYPE 4

Which figure is the odd one out?

ODD ONE OUT

A   B   C   D   E

Answer = E

Rule 1 = the sequence follows the rule of alternation.

Rule 2 = the sequence follows the pattern of one square being on the top of the horizontal line, and one square being on the bottom of the horizontal line.

Figure E is the odd one out because the figure only contains two squares underneath the horizontal line, whereas all of the horizontal lines on the other figures have one square on top, and one square on the bottom.

For questions like these, you need to pay careful attention to what is changing. You need to distinguish what figure is the 'odd one out' by determining the differences. This could be based on reflections, rotations, alternations etc.

Note, we have highlighted what is missing in Figure E to give you a better understanding of what you need to look for in this particular question.

QUESTION TYPE 5

Which of the cubes can be made from the cube net?

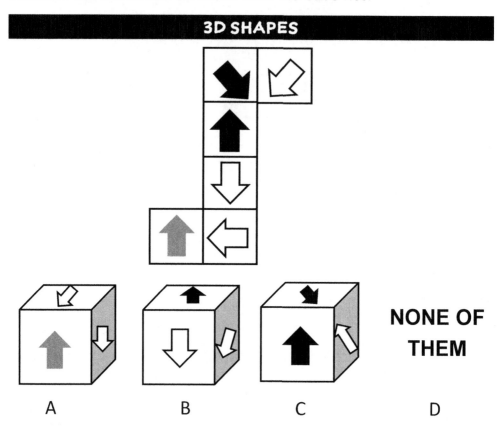

3D SHAPES

A   B   C   D

NONE OF THEM

Answer = D

For these types of questions, you need to make sure that you fold along the creases of the cube net, so that the shapes remain on the outside of the cube.

Top Tip! If you struggle with these types of questions and find it difficult to imagine what the cube would look like, why don't you make a cube using a piece of paper. Make a cube net, draw on the shapes, and see what it looks like!

Practising these questions in this way will allow these questions to become easier by having something to visualise. These types of questions, given time and practice, will become much easier to visualise in your head, and eventually you won't have to rely on drawing them out every time!

QUESTION TYPE 6

Which of the Answer Figures fits in with the Question Figures?

QUESTION AND ANSWER FIGURES

Question Figures

Answer Figures

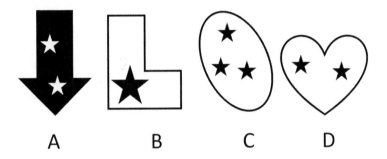

A   B   C   D

Answer = D

Rule 1 = the shape must contain two stars inside a large white shape.

The heart shape is the only figure which follows the pattern above. Therefore answer option D is the correct answer.

QUESTION TYPE 7

The middle row of boxes create a rule that has been applied to the boxes directly above them. Which answer option (A to E) corresponds to the rule under the box with the question mark?

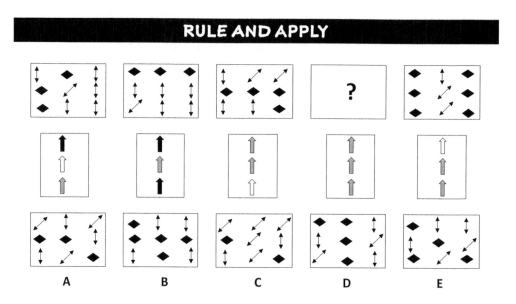

RULE AND APPLY

A   B   C   D   E

Answer = A

Rule 1 = The rule in this question sees the number of grey arrows dictating the number of diagonal arrows in the pattern above.

Rule 2 = The rule being applied to box with the question mark means that three diagonal arrows should appear in the answer.

INDUCTIVE REASONING STRATEGIES

- Questions will often require you to identi shapes in regards to how they can be linked. The shapes or figures are often linked or connected in some way, so it is important not to get distracted by irrelevant information you have been given.

- Make sure you are continuously referring to strategic methods to work out the questions. Issues in size, colours, numbers, sides, positioning, shading, symmetry, angles, direction etc, all need to be considered when trying to work out each question.

- Do not spend too much time on one particular question. You may find some questions easier than others. You may struggle at a certain 'type' of question and so it is important not to ponder about questions you are unsure of. Move on and then come back to those questions at the end.

- Remember to read each question carefully and understand what it is asking you.

- Try and visualise the questions!

- Accuracy is key. You need to remain as accurate as possible to ensure successful marks. That's why it is important to fully comprehend the questions and understand what is being asked.

- Inductive Reasoning tests are designed to test people under strict time limits. Most people find it difficult to finish all the questions. Do not be put off by the thought of not completing the whole test. These tests are designed to make it hard for candidates to finish. Psychometric testing is fundamentally used to measure people's level of accuracy, whilst working in speedy conditions.

- It is not wrong to draw out your answers as you go along. Drawing out the answers of what you think it may look like, may help you to visualise the answers more clearly.

- It is often said that using highlighters are a useful way to distinguish your answers. Highlighting is helpful if you are counting lots of shapes or working out lots of numbers or angles etc.

- Within the 'complete the sequence' questions, you can always work backwards, in order to make sure you have the correct answer. By working backwards, you will have to do the opposite of what is being asked, but this is sometimes a useful tip if you are struggling with the conventional methods.

- Practice is key. If you struggle with visualising shapes and objects, you may struggle with these tests. This is why we have provided you with plenty of sample questions for you to work through. The more you practice these tests, the more likely you are to feel comfortable and confident with the questions. Remember, practice makes perfect!

- If you are unsure about the answers, make sure you use our detailed answers and explanations to understand how to get to the correct answer. Remember, knowing where you went wrong is just as important as getting the questions correct. You need to understand how the answer can be reached. Try practising the question again after reading through the answers and explanations to ensure you know where you went wrong.

- Check out our free online psychometric testing and sample questions to ensure you are fully prepared for your Inductive Reasoning test.

www.PsychometricTestsOnline.co.uk

TIPS FOR PASSING INDUCTIVE REASONING TESTS

Look at one aspect at a time.

- Try not to look at the whole image; break it down and determine what is going on. You will feel overwhelmed in the test if you try to decipher the image holistically. You should 'decode' the image and break it down into smaller sections; that way you will be able to visualise what is going on. Study carefully, one aspect at a time!

You can always work backwards!

- If you get stuck, why not try the sequence in reverse. This will allow you to visualise the sequence from a different perspective, and allow you to spot something you may have missed previously.

Practice!

- No great accomplishment comes easy! You have to work hard at it! Perseverance and practice are two important things to remember when sitting an Inductive Reasoning test. Nothing will boost your chances at success more than if you practice them prior to your real test. Not only will this give you clarity and understanding in regards of what to expect, but it will also take off some of the pressure you may be feeling before that all important test!

Stay calm.

- If you lose focus or become overwhelmed during your Inductive Reasoning test, it is highly likely that this will impact your overall performance. The Inductive Reasoning tests are timed, and this time limit is quite constraining, therefore it is important to stay calm and assured to ensure accurate results.

Manage your time.

- The time you are allowed to complete your Inductive Reasoning test will very much depend on your circumstances. Try to find out how long your test is going to last, and use this information to your advantage. If you take on board the tip about practising, you will be able to practice your timing skills beforehand. Managing your time in psychometric tests is significant; practising these tests prior to your real test will give you some indication of how well you will perform under strict time restrictions.

Now move on to the next section of the guide.

INDUCTIVE REASONING
SECTION 1

QUESTION 1

What figure completes the sequence pattern?

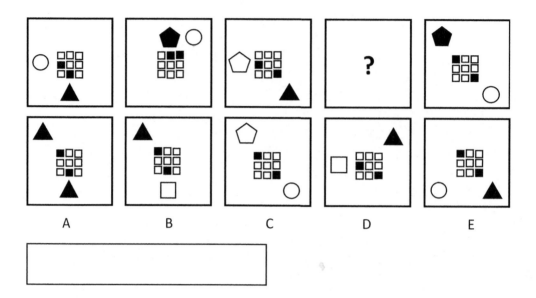

QUESTION 2

What figure completes the sequence pattern?

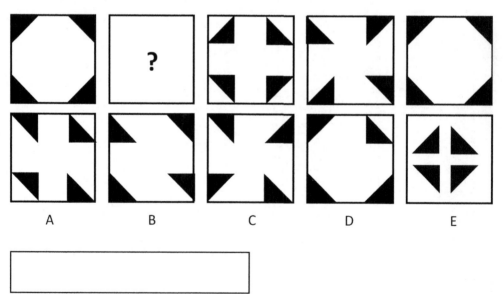

QUESTION 3

What figure completes the sequence pattern?

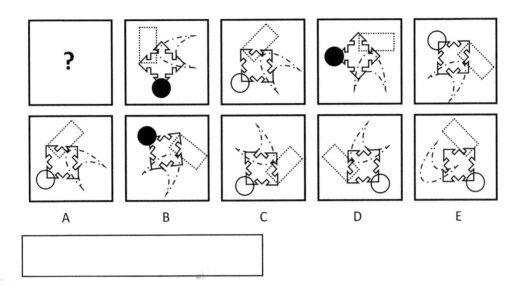

A   B   C   D   E

QUESTION 4

What figure completes the sequence pattern?

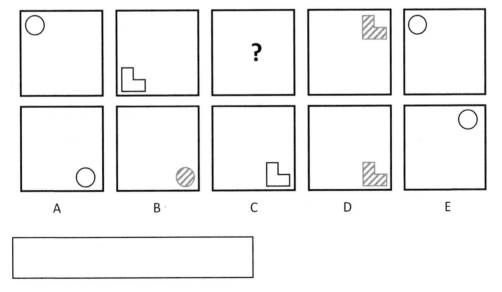

A   B   C   D   E

QUESTION 5

What figure completes the sequence pattern?

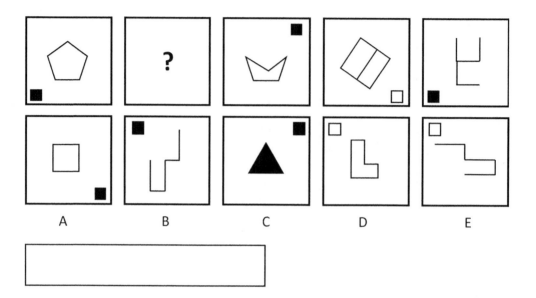

QUESTION 6

What figure completes the sequence pattern?

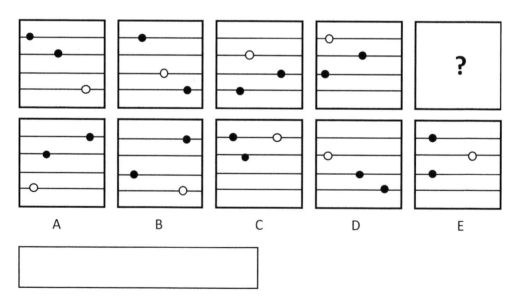

QUESTION 7

What figure completes the sequence pattern?

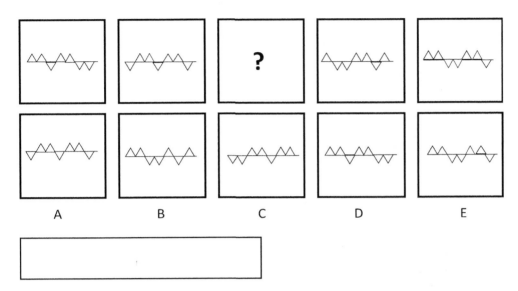

A   B   C   D   E

QUESTION 8

What figure completes the sequence pattern?

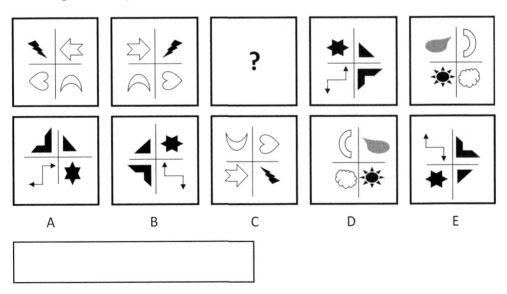

A   B   C   D   E

QUESTION 9

What figure completes the sequence pattern?

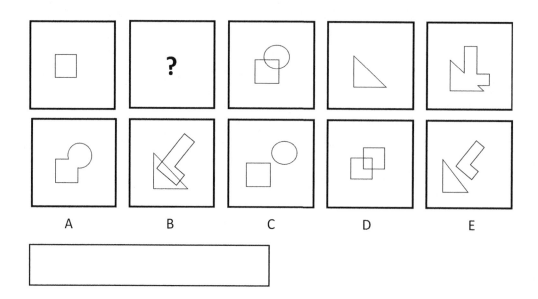

QUESTION 10

What figure completes the sequence pattern?

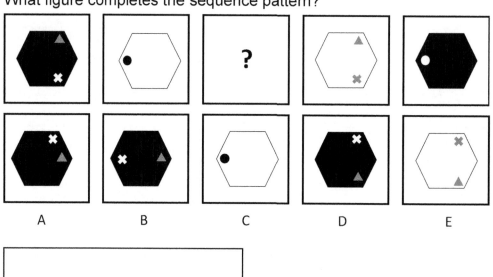

QUESTION 11

What figure completes the sequence pattern?

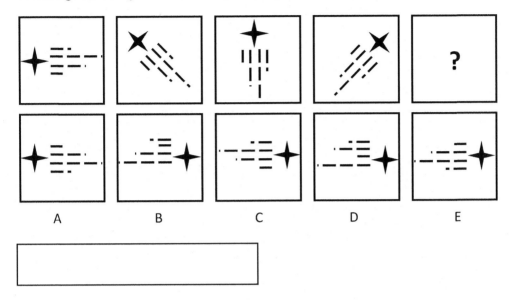

QUESTION 12

What figure completes the sequence pattern?

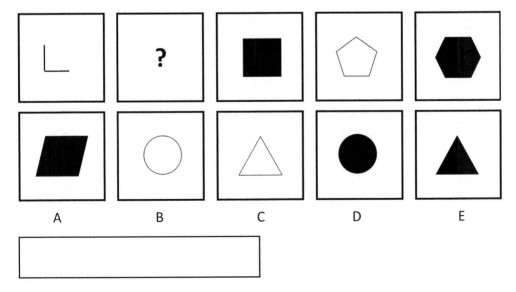

QUESTION 13

What figure completes the sequence pattern?

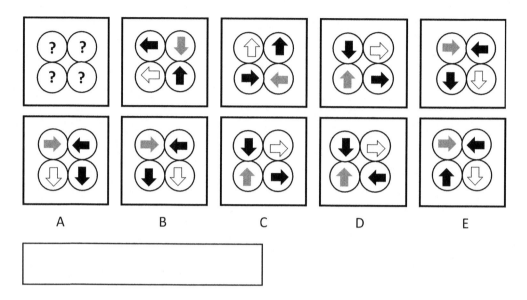

A   B   C   D   E

QUESTION 14

What figure completes the sequence pattern?

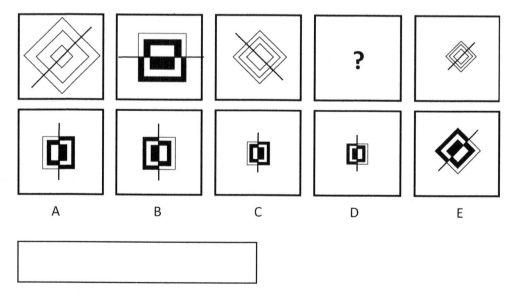

A   B   C   D   E

QUESTION 15

What figure completes the sequence pattern?

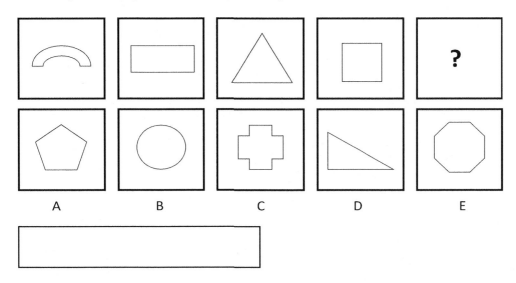

QUESTION 16

What figure completes the sequence pattern?

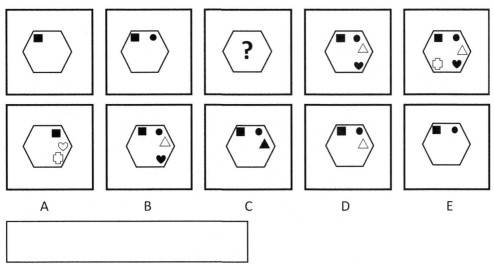

QUESTION 17

What figure completes the sequence pattern?

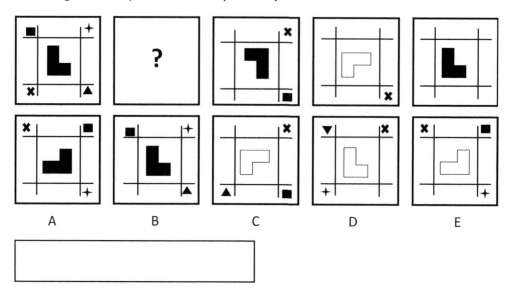

QUESTION 18

What figure completes the sequence pattern?

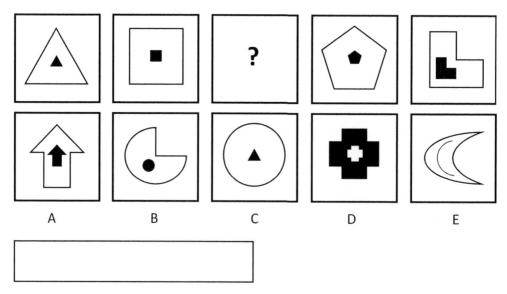

QUESTION 19

What figure completes the sequence pattern?

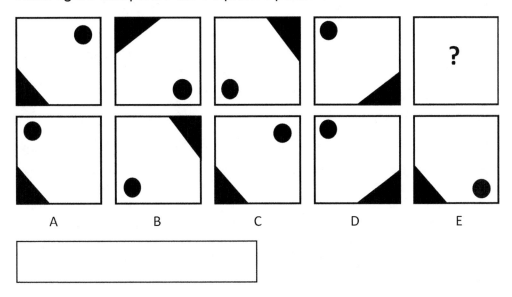

QUESTION 20

What figure completes the sequence pattern?

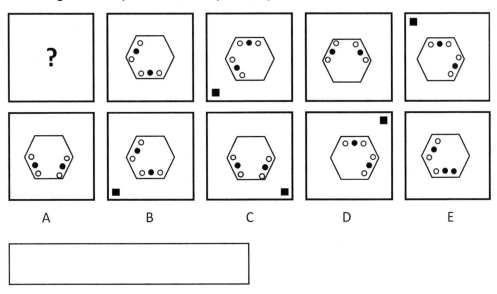

ANSWERS TO SECTION 1

Q1. B

Rule 1 = the large shape's position is determined by the small, black squares.

Rule 2 = for the large shapes; one shape has to be white, and the other has to be black.

Figure A can be ruled out because both the large shapes are black; there should be one large shape that is white. Figure C can be ruled out because both the large shapes are white; there should be one large shape that is black. Figure D can be ruled out because the black triangle should be positioned at the bottom right corner (the small black square determines the place of the large shape). Figure E can be ruled out because the white circle should be positioned at the top left corner (the small black square determines the place of the large shape).

Q2. C

Rule 1 = each shaded triangle has been rotated 90° clockwise.

Figure A can be ruled out because the triangle in the top right corner needs to be rotated 90° anti-clockwise; the triangle in the bottom left corner needs to be rotated 90° anti-clockwise. Figure B can be ruled out because all the triangles have been rotated incorrectly. Figure D can be ruled out because all of the triangles have been rotated incorrectly. Figure E can be ruled out because it is a replica of box 3 in the sequence; it has just been condensed.

Q3. D

Rule 1 = the whole shape is being rotated 45° clockwise. The figure in box 1 is a 45° rotation into box 2. Box 2 is a 45° rotation into box 3 and so forth.

Figure A can be ruled out because it is a replica of the image in box 2. Figure B can be ruled out because it is a replica of box 5. Figure C can be ruled out because it is a reflection of what the answer should be. Figure E can be ruled out because the rectangle and moon-shape have swapped places.

Q4. B

Rule 1 = the shapes move one corner anti-clockwise as the sequence progresses.

Rule 2 = the shapes alternate from a circle to an 'L' shape.

Rule 3 = the colour pattern alternates from white, white, patterned, patterned and repeats.

Figure A can be ruled out because the circle needs to be shaded as opposed to being white. Figure C can be ruled out because it needs to be a shaded circle as opposed to a white 'L' shape. Figure D can be ruled out because it needs to be a patterned circle as opposed to a patterned 'L' shape. Figure E can be ruled out because the circle needs to be patterned and in the bottom right corner as opposed to the top right corner.

Q5. E

Rule 1 = the small square moves around one place clockwise as the sequence progresses.

Rule 2 = the small square alternates from black to white as the sequence progresses.

Rule 3 = the shape in the centre must contain five sides.

Figure A can be ruled out because the shape in the centre has only four sides; also, the black square in the bottom right corner should be a white square in the top left corner. Figure B can be ruled out because the black square needs to be a white square. Figure C can be ruled out because the shape in the centre needs to be five sides; also the black square in the top right corner needs to be a white square in the top left corner. Figure D can be ruled out because the shape in the centre has six sides, and it should have five sides.

Q6. A

Rule 1 = the two black dots remain straight after one another (there is no line in between the two black dots).

Rule 2 = the white dot remains one line ahead of the last black dot.

Rule 3 = the dots move up one line each time.

Figure B can be ruled out because the black dots should not have a line in between them. Figure C can be ruled out because the black dot should not be on the same line as the white dot. Figure D can be ruled out because the white dot needs to be on the bottom line. Figure E can be ruled out because the two black dots have been separated by the white dot in the middle.

Q7. C

Rule 1 = the triangles move one place to the right as the sequence progresses.

Rule 2 = once the triangle reaches the end of the horizontal line, the triangle is placed back at the start.

Figure A can be ruled out because it is a replica of box 2. Figure B can be ruled out because the triangles at the end of the figure are incorrect. Figure D can be ruled out because it is a replica of box 1. Figure E can be ruled out because it is a replica of box 5.

Q8. B

Rule 1 = the sequence is all about vertical reflections.

Rule 2 = box 1 is reflected to box 2. Box 3 is reflected to box 4 and so on. Figure A can be ruled out because this has been reflected and then rotated; it is not a mere reflection of the next box. Figure C can be ruled out because this is a horizontal reflection of box 2; we want a reflection of box 4. Figure D can be ruled out because this is a vertical reflection of box 5; we want a vertical reflection of box 4. Figure E can be ruled out because this is a horizontal reflection of box 4; we want a vertical reflection of box 4.

Q9. A

Rule 1 = to get from box 1 to box 2, the shapes need to merge. It uses one shape (in box 1); and you have to work out which shape it is being merged with (in this case it is a square and a circle). The third box indicates which two shapes have been merged together and demonstrates the overlap.

Rule 2 = after the first three boxes, the sequence begins again with different shapes but following the same rule.

Figure B can be ruled out because the shapes merging together need to be a square and a circle. Figure C can be ruled out because two shapes need to be merged as opposed to separate. Figure D can be ruled out because the two shapes need to be a circle and a square; and not two squares. Figure E can be ruled out because the shapes need to be a circle and a square; not a triangle and an 'L' shape.

Q10. D

Rule 1 = the large hexagon alternates between black and white as the sequence progresses.

Rule 2 = the grey triangle moves two points anti-clockwise around the hexagon as the sequence progresses.

Rule 3 = the small cross moves two points clockwise around the hexagon as the sequence progresses.

Rule 4 = if the triangle and the cross coincide, the shapes become a black circle (if on a white hexagon) or a white circle (if on a black hexagon).

Figures A, B, C and E all have one or more shapes in the incorrect position and therefore cannot follow the sequence.

Q11. E

Rule 1 = the whole shape is being rotated 45° clockwise. The figure in box 1 is a 45° rotation into box 2. Box 2 is a 45° rotation into box 3 and so forth.

Figure A can be ruled out because it is a horizontal reflection of box A. Figure B can be ruled out because the line on the top should be at the bottom. Figure C can be ruled out because it is a vertical reflection of box A. Figure D can be ruled out because the lines have been positioned in different places.

Q12. C

Rule 1 = the sequence adds one side to the previous shape, as the sequence progresses. For example, a triangle (3 sides), turns into a square (4 sides) and so forth.

Rule 2 = the sequence alternates colour pattern between black and white.

Figure A can be ruled out because the shape needs to be 3-sided, not 4-sided. Figure B can be ruled out because the shape needs to be 3-sided, not a circle. Figure D can be ruled out because the shape needs to be 3-sided and white, not a circle and black. Figure E can be ruled out because it needs to be a white triangle, not a black triangle.

Q13. B

Rule 1 = the whole shape rotates 90° clockwise.

Figure A can be ruled out because the white and black arrows pointing downwards have swapped places. Figure C can be ruled out because this is a replica of box 4. Figure D can be ruled out because none of the arrows are in the correct position. Figure E can be ruled out because the black arrow pointing upwards should be pointing downwards.

Q14. B

Rule 1 = the whole shape is being rotated 45° clockwise. The figure in box 1 is a 45° rotation into box 2. Box 2 is a 45° rotation into box 3 and so forth. Rule 2 = each figure gets smaller than the previous.

Figure A can be ruled out because it is a reflection of what the answer should look like. Figure C can be ruled out because it is the wrong size and has been reflected. Figure D can be ruled out because it is the wrong size. Figure E can be ruled out because it should only be rotated 45° from the previous box (instead it has been rotated an extra 45°).

Q15. A

Rule 1 = each shape adds another line of symmetry. For example, the first shape (the rainbow shape) has 1 line of symmetry, the second shape (the rectangle) has 2 lines of symmetry and so forth.

Figure B can be ruled out because a circle will look the same no matter how many times you rotate it. Figure C can be ruled out because it has 4 lines of symmetry. Figure D can be ruled out because this triangle has no line of symmetry. Figure E can be ruled out because this has 8 lines of symmetry.

Q16. D

Rule 1 = in each of the corners of the hexagon, a shape is placed.

Rule 2 = these shapes start in the top left corner and are added in a clockwise manner.

Figure A can be ruled out because we are looking for a black square, a black circle and a white triangle. Figure B can be ruled out because we only need three shapes, not four. Figure C can be ruled out because the triangle needs to be white, not black. Figure E can be ruled out because we need three shapes, not two.

Q17. E

Rule 1 = the shape in the middle rotates 90° anti-clockwise as the sequence progresses.

Rule 2 = the shape in the middle alternates from black to white as the sequence progresses.

Rule 3 = the small shapes move one position to the next corner (in a clockwise manner).

Rule 4 = as the shapes rotate around, a shape is removed. You will notice that the 'cross' shape appears the most. Therefore, this must be the beginning of this sequence, and so the last shape rotated (using the 'cross' to begin) will be removed.

Figure A can be ruled out because the shape in the middle needs to be white, not black. Figure B can be ruled out because the shape in the middle needs to be white, and rotated 90° anti-clockwise. Also, the small shapes do not follow the correct pattern. Figure C can be ruled out because the shape in the middle needs to be rotated 180°. Also the small shapes do not follow the correct pattern. Figure D can be ruled out because the shape in the middle needs to be rotated 90° anti-clockwise. None of the small shapes are in the correct position.

Q18. A

Rule 1 = the large shape is white. The small shapes are black.

Rule 2 = the small shape inside the large shape is the same shape.

Figure B can be ruled out because the 'pac-man' shape does not contain the same shape in the centre of the shape, it contains a circle instead. Figure C can be ruled out because the large white circle should contain a small black circle, not a black triangle. Figure D can be ruled out because the large shape should be white, and the small shape should be black. Figure E can be ruled out because the moon shape only contains a curved line, not a small moon shape.

Q19. C

Rule 1 = the shapes move 90° clockwise as the sequence progresses.

Figure A can be ruled out because the black dot should be in the top right corner, not the top left. Figure B can be ruled out because the black dot and black triangle should be in one another's place. Figure D can be ruled out because the dot and the triangle need to be moved one corner clockwise. Figure E can be ruled out because the black dot needs to be in the top right corner, not the bottom right.

Q20. C

Rule 1 = the dots move to one side in a clockwise motion.

Rule 2 = every other figure in the sequence contains a black square in the corner of the whole box. This square moves one corner clockwise.

Figure A can be ruled out because the figure does not contain a black square in the bottom right corner. Figure B can be ruled out because the dots are not in the correct position. They need to be positioned so that the side that is empty and in between the two lines of dots is at the bottom. The black square should be in the bottom right corner, not the bottom left. Figure D can be ruled out because the side that is empty and in between the two lines of dots should be at the bottom, not at the top right side. The black square should be in the bottom right corner, not the top right. Figure E can be ruled out because the side that is empty and in between the two lines of dots, should be bottom centre, not bottom left. The figure also needs to contain a black square in the bottom right corner.

INDUCTIVE REASONING
SECTION 2

QUESTION 1

What figure comes next in the series?

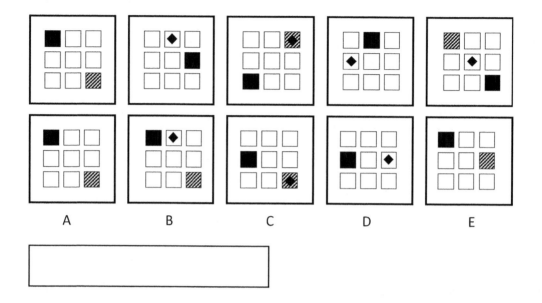

QUESTION 2

What figure comes next in the series?

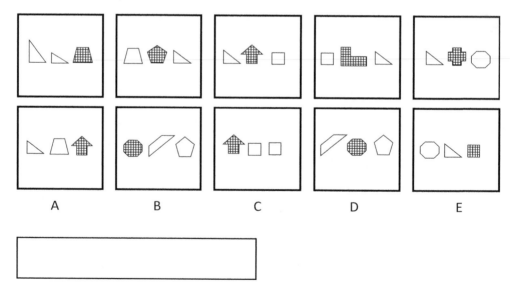

QUESTION 3

What figure comes next in the series?

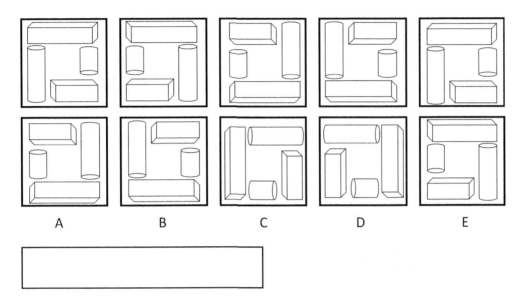

A   B   C   D   E

QUESTION 4

What figure comes next in the series?

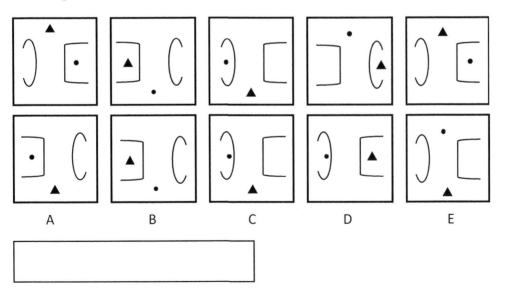

A   B   C   D   E

QUESTION 5

What figure comes next in the series?

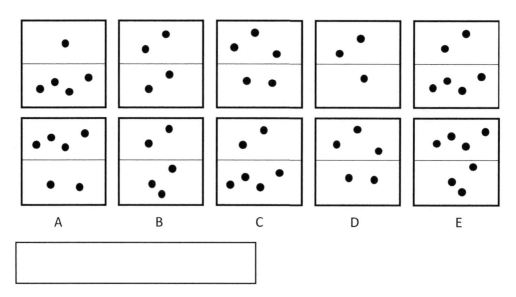

QUESTION 6

What figure comes next in the series?

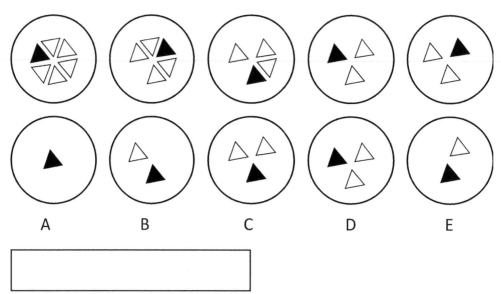

QUESTION 7

What figure comes next in the series?

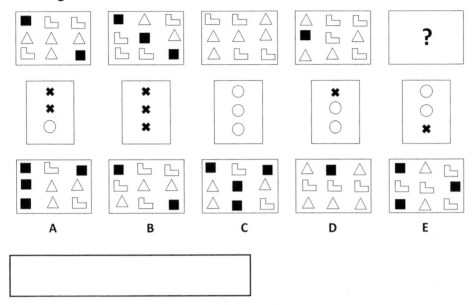

QUESTION 8

What figure comes next in the series?

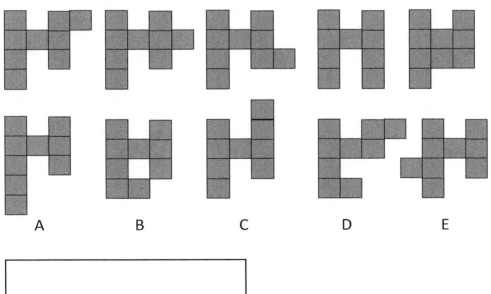

QUESTION 9

What figure comes next in the series?

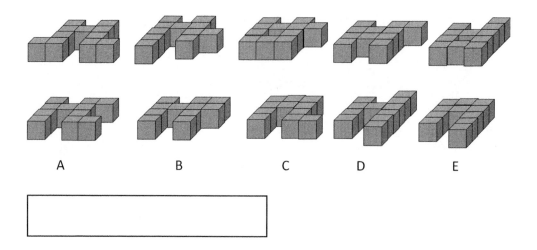

A   B   C   D   E

QUESTION 10

What figure comes next in the series?

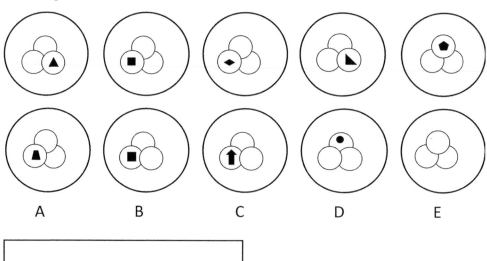

A   B   C   D   E

QUESTION 11

What figure comes next in the series?

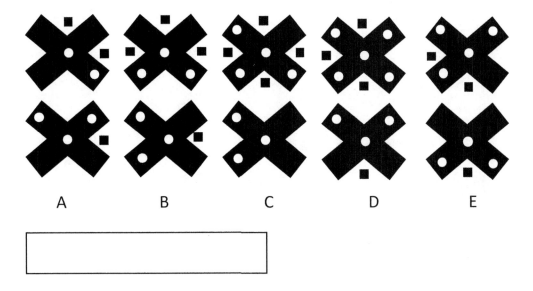

A   B   C   D   E

QUESTION 12

What figure comes next in the series?

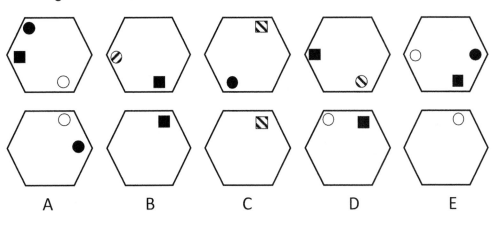

A   B   C   D   E

QUESTION 13

What figure comes next in the series?

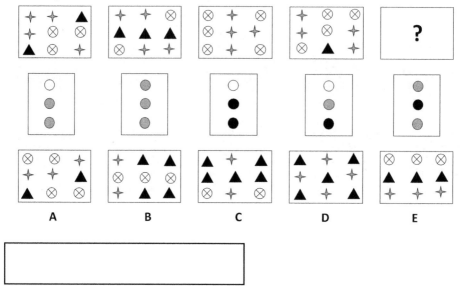

QUESTION 14

What figure comes next in the series?

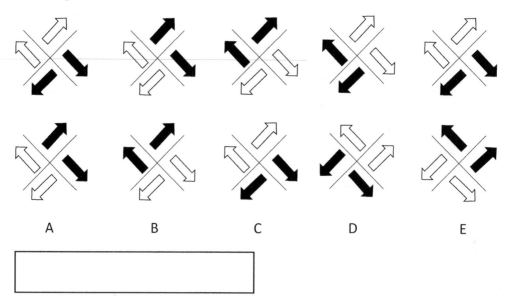

QUESTION 15

What figure comes next in the series?

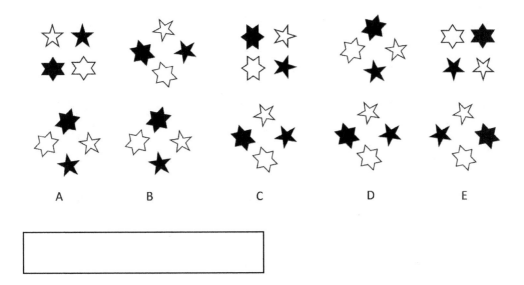

QUESTION 16

What figure comes next in the series?

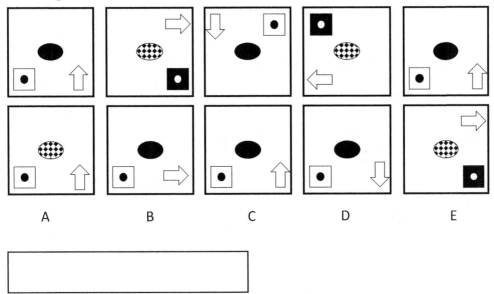

QUESTION 17

What figure comes next in the series?

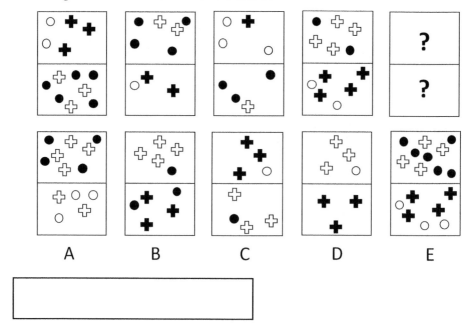

A   B   C   D   E

QUESTION 18

What figure comes next in the series?

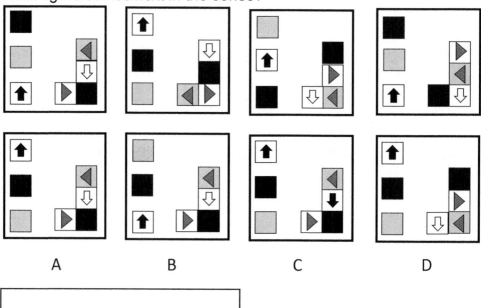

A   B   C   D

QUESTION 19

What figure comes next in the series?

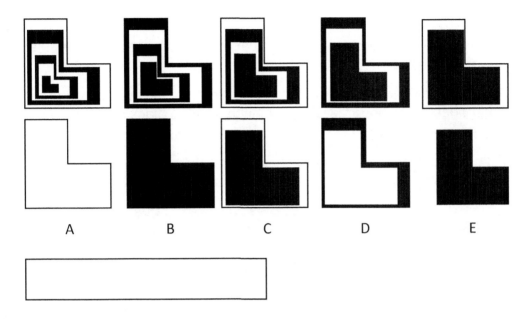

A	B	C	D	E

QUESTION 20

What figure comes next in the series?

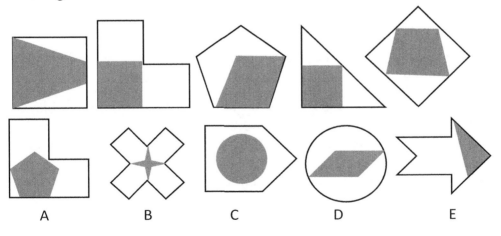

A	B	C	D	E

ANSWERS TO SECTION 2

Q1. D

Rule 1 = the black square moves 3 spaces clockwise, around the outer edge of the squares.

Rule 2 = the shaded box moves one space anti-clockwise, around the outer edge of the squares. If this coincides with a black square, it turns into a black square.

Rule 3 = the black diamond moves along the sequence from left to right; and once it reaches the end, it begins on the next row.

Figure A can be ruled out because the black square needs to be the first square on the second row. The shaded square should have disappeared and the black diamond should be the third square on the second row. Figure B can be ruled out because none of the shaded or black squares are in the correct place. The diamond shape is also in the incorrect position. Figure C can be ruled out because the diamond should be the third square on the second row. The shaded box should have disappeared. Figure E can be ruled out because the black square needs to be on the row underneath; the shaded box should have disappeared and instead, have a black diamond in it.

Q2. B

Rule 1 = the last shape in each figure begins the shape in the next box.
Rule 2 = the shape with the most sides is highlighted.

Figure A can be ruled out because the sequence must start with an octagon, not a triangle. Figure C can be ruled out because the first shape in the sequence needs to be an octagon as opposed to an arrow. Figure D can be ruled out because the sequence needs to start with an octagon. Figure E can be ruled out because the octagon needs to be shaded in (it has the most number of sides in that figure).

Q3. E

Rule 1 = the sequence follows a vertical reflection, then a horizontal reflection, vertical reflection, horizontal reflection and so forth.

Figure A can be ruled out because it has been reflected horizontally from box 2. Figure B can be ruled out because it has been reflected horizontally, not vertically. Figure C can be ruled out because it has been rotated, and then reflected horizontally. Figure D can be ruled out because it has been rotated 90° anti-clockwise from box 5.

Q4. B

Rule 1 = the two shapes like brackets are rotated 180° each time as the sequence progresses.

Rule 2 = the black dot moves one place around the square in a clockwise manner.

Rule 3 = the black triangle rotates one place around the square in an anti- clockwise manner.

Figure A can be ruled out because the triangle and the dot should be in each other's position. Figure C can be ruled out because the brackets are in the wrong position. The black dot and triangle also need to be in each other's position. Figure D can be ruled out because the brackets are in the wrong position. Also, the black dot should be at the bottom in the middle, and the triangle should be middle left. Figure E can be ruled out because the brackets are in the wrong position. The triangle should be middle left and the black dot should be at the bottom in the middle.

Q5. B

Rule 1 = working from the top half of the box, using a zig-zag method across the sequence, the dots follow the pattern of: 1, 2, 3, 1, 2, 3 and so on.

Rule 2 = working from the bottom half of the box, using a zig-zag method across the sequence, the dots follow the pattern of: 4, 2, 2, 2, 4, 2, 2 and so on.

Figure A can be ruled out because the top box needs 2 dots, and the bottom of the box needs 3 dots. Figure C can be ruled out because the bottom half of the box should have 3 dots, not 4. Figure D can be ruled out because the top half of the box needs 2 dots and the bottom half needs 3 dots. Figure E can be ruled out because the top half of the box needs 2 dots, not 4 dots.

Q6. C

Rule 1 = the black triangle moves two places clockwise around the figure. Rule 2 = the triangle opposite the black triangle, disappears.

Rule 3 = using the previous figure, the triangles that have already disappeared, remain disappeared. The triangle opposite the black triangle will then be taken off.

Figure A can be ruled out because no more triangles can be taken off the sequence. The sequence repeats itself, only alternating where the black triangle is; it cannot take off any more triangles. Figure B can be ruled out because no more triangles can disappear. Figure D can be ruled out because the black triangle should be at the bottom of the figure, not the top left. Figure E can be ruled out because no more triangles can disappear from the sequence.

Q7. D

The rule in this question sees the black crosses dictating the number of squares in the pattern above. The rule being applied to box with the question mark means that only one black square should appear in the answer.

Q8. B

Rule 1 = using the square at the top right (last square on the first row); this square moves one place around the outer edge of the overall shape. It circulates the overall shape in a clockwise manner.

Figure A can be ruled out because the fifth square in the first column should be on the fourth row, second column. Figure C can be ruled out because the first square on the first row, should be on the fifth row, second column. Figure D can be ruled out because the third square on the first row, should be on the third row, third column. Figure E can be ruled out because the square on the third row, first column, should be on the fourth row, third column.

Q9. E

Rule 1 = the last square on the bottom row circulates around the object, one space at a time, anti-clockwise.

Rule 2 = the first square on the bottom row circulates around the object, one space at a time, anti-clockwise.

Figure A can be ruled out because the last square on the first row should fill the gap on the first row. The last square on the bottom row should be at the bottom in the third column. Figure B can be ruled out because both squares in the fourth column are in the wrong position. Figure C can be ruled out because the last square on the bottom row should be the last square in the third column. Figure D can be ruled out because the first square in the first row should fill the gap in the second row.

Q10. A

Rule 1 = the circle that is at the front should contain a small shape.

Rule 2 = the small shape in the circle (at the front) needs to be black.

Figure B can be ruled out because the circle containing the black shape is not at the front. Figure C can be ruled out because the circle containing the black shape is not at the front. Figure D can be ruled out because the circle containing the black shape is not at the front. Figure E can be ruled out because it doesn't contain a small shape.

Q11. D

Rule 1 = a white dot gets added each time. This dot is added in a clockwise manner, until all the corners of the cross are filled.

Rule 2 = once the white dots fill all the corners, the dots then disappear in the same clockwise manner.

Rule 3 = the black squares follows a similar pattern. The square gets added in the grooves of the cross in an anti-clockwise manner.

Rule 4 = once the black square occupies all the grooves, the square then disappears in the same anti-clockwise manner.

Figure A can be ruled out because the square should be at the bottom of the cross, not on the right side. Figure B can be ruled out because the bottom left dot should be placed at the top right of the cross. The black square should be at the bottom of the cross. Figure C can be ruled out because the bottom left dot should be at the top right of the cross. A black square needs to be added at the bottom of the cross. Figure E can be ruled out because the bottom left dot should be top left; and the bottom right dot should be top right of the cross.

Q12. C

Rule 1 = the black dot moves one space anti-clockwise as the sequence progresses.

Rule 2 = the white dot moves two spaces clockwise as the sequence progresses.

Rule 3 = if the white dot coincides with the black dot, the black dot becomes patterned.

Rule 4 = the black square moves two spaces anti-clockwise as the sequence progresses.

Rule 5 = if the black square coincides with either circle, is becomes a patterned square.

Figure A can be ruled out because the white circle should be a black patterned square. The black circle should disappear. Figure B can be ruled out because the black square should be patterned. Figure D can be ruled out because the white circle should disappear. Figure E can be ruled out because the white circle should be a black patterned square.

Q13. A

The rule in this question sees the grey circles dictating the number of black triangles in the pattern above. The rule being applied to box with the question mark means that two black triangles should appear in the answer.

Q14. A

Rule 1 = the figures have been rotated 90° anti-clockwise.

Figure B can be ruled out because it has been rotated 180°. Figure C can be ruled out because this is the same figure as the previous figure in the sequence. Figure D can be ruled out because this has been reflected horizontally from box 3. Figure E can be ruled out because this has been reflected vertically from box 3.

Q15. C

Rule 1 = the figures have been rotated 45° clockwise.

Figure A can be ruled out because this is rotated approximately 45°

anti- clockwise. Figure B can be ruled out because this is a reflection of what the answer should look like. Figure D can be ruled out because this has not been rotated 45° clockwise. Figure E can be ruled out because the two white stars are in the wrong position.

Q16. E

Rule 1 = the white rectangle with the black dot moves around the square anti- clockwise, and alternates colours from black to white.

Rule 2 = the black oval in the middle alternates from black to patterned.

Rule 3 = the white arrow rotates 90° clockwise and moves around the square anti-clockwise.

You will notice that box 4 is repeating box 1. Therefore, the next figure in the series should repeat the same as the figure in box 2.

Q17. C

Rule 1 = in the top half of the first box, and using a zig-zag method across the sequence, it contains 3 black crosses and 2 white dots, this decreases by 1 each time, until it reaches the end whereby the sequence starts again.

Rule 2 = in the bottom half of the first box, and using a zig-zag method across the sequence, it contains 3 white crosses and 5 black dots. This decreases by 1 each time, until it reaches the end whereby the sequence starts again.

Figure A can be ruled out because the top half of the box should contain 3 black crosses and 1 white dot. The bottom half of the box should contain 3 white crosses and 1 black dot. Figure B can be ruled out because the colours and numbers of shapes in each half of the box are incorrect. Figure D can be ruled out because the top half of the box should have 3 black crosses, not 3 white crosses. The bottom half of the box should contain a white dot. Figure E can be ruled out because the top box should contain 3 black crosses and 1 black dot; and the bottom half of the box should contain 3 white crosses and a black dot.

Q18. A

Rule 1 = within each square of the series, the 3 squares to the left move down one as the sequence progresses.

Rule 2 = within each square of the series, the 4 shapes to the right move up one as the sequence progresses

Q19. B

Rule 1 = the sequence alternates colours from black to white. For example, black shapes will turn into white shapes and vice versa.

Rule 2 = as the sequence progresses, the shapes in the middle disappear.

Figure A can be ruled out because it needs to be a black shape not a white shape. Figure C can be ruled out because there should only be one 'L' shape and not two. Figure D can be ruled out because there should only be one 'L' shape and not two. Figure E can be ruled out because, although it is a black 'L' shape, the sizing is incorrect; we should be left with the large 'L' shape.

Q20. D

Rule 1 = the shaded shape inside the larger shape should contain four sides.

Figure A can be ruled out because the shaded shape has five sides instead of four. Figure B can be ruled out because the shaded shape has eight sides instead of four. Figure C can be ruled out because the shaded shape is a circle and therefore only has a circumference as opposed to sides. Figure E can be ruled out because the shaded shape has three sides instead of four.

INDUCTIVE REASONING
SECTION 3

QUESTION 1

Which figure is the odd one out?

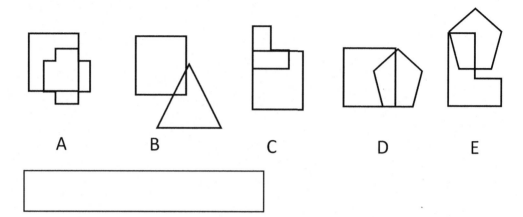

A B C D E

QUESTION 2

What comes next in the sequence?

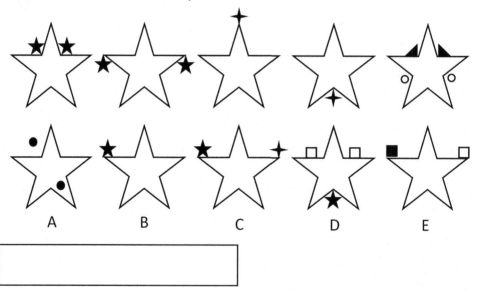

A B C D E

QUESTION 3

Which answer fits in with the sequence?

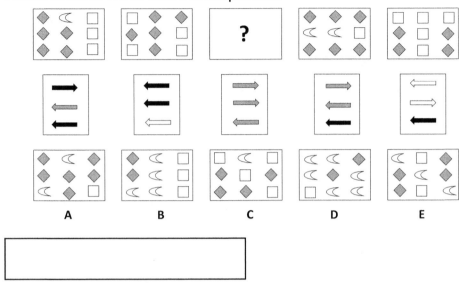

QUESTION 4

What comes next in the sequence?

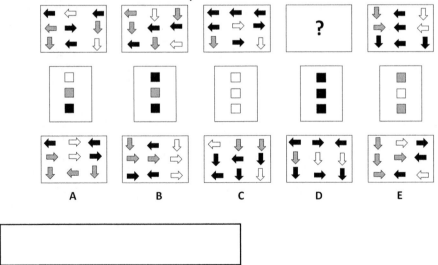

QUESTION 5

What completes the sequence?

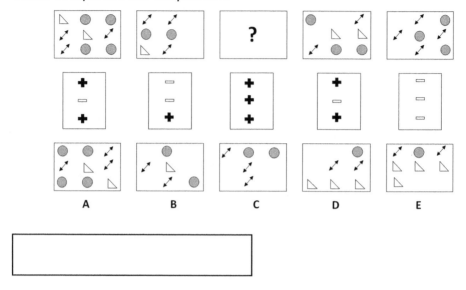

QUESTION 6

What comes next in the sequence?

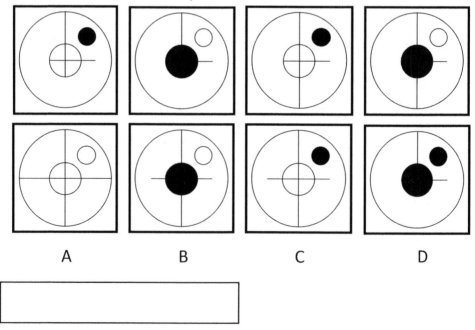

QUESTION 7

What comes next in the sequence?

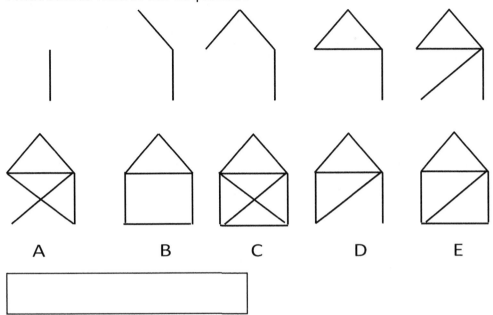

A	B	C	D	E

QUESTION 8

Which answer fits in with the sequence?

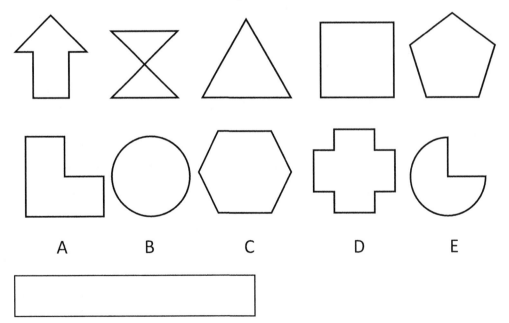

A	B	C	D	E

QUESTION 9

What comes next in the sequence?

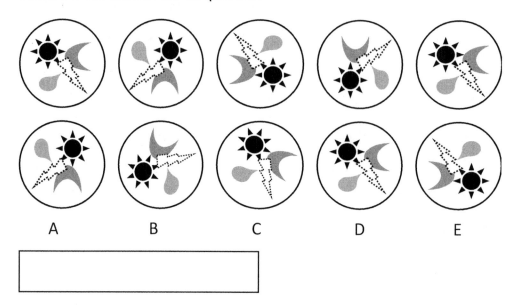

QUESTION 10

What comes next in the sequence?

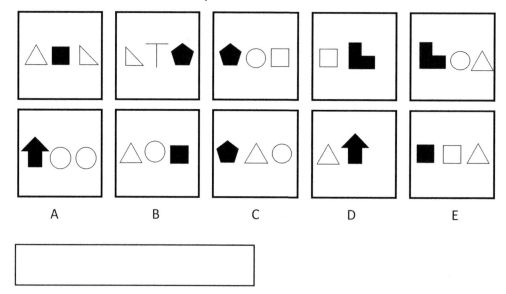

QUESTION 11

What comes next in the sequence?

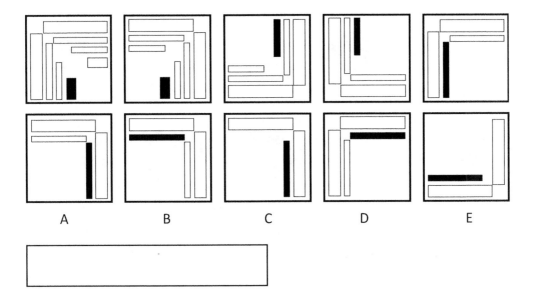

| A | B | C | D | E |

QUESTION 12

Which answer fits in with the sequence?

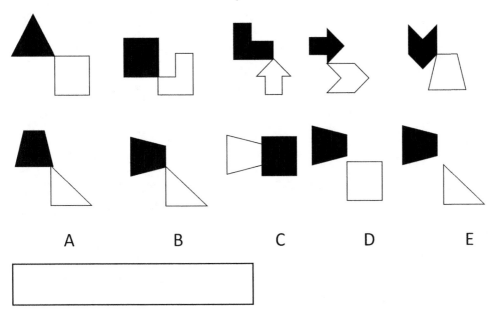

| A | B | C | D | E |

QUESTION 13

Which answer fits in with the sequence?

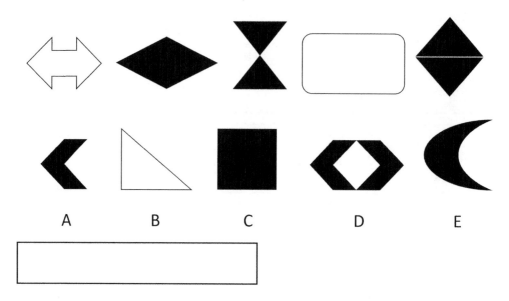

A B C D E

QUESTION 14

What completes the sequence?

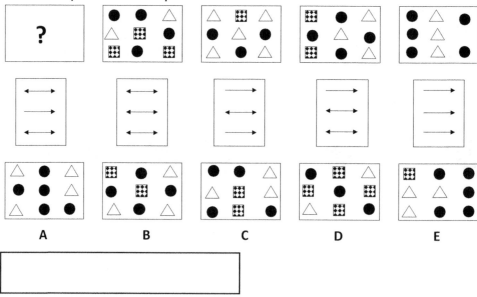

A B C D E

QUESTION 15

What comes next in the sequence?

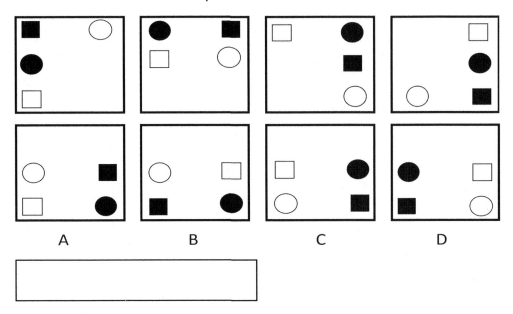

A	B	C	D

QUESTION 16

What comes next in the sequence?

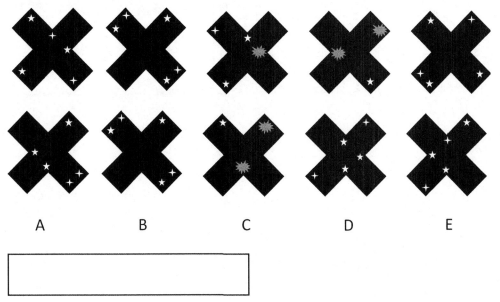

A	B	C	D	E

QUESTION 17

What comes next in the sequence?

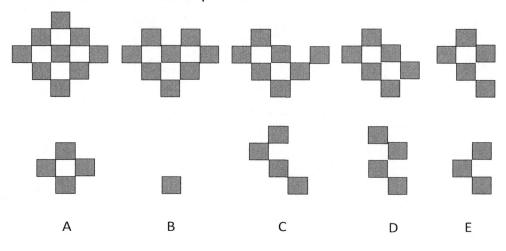

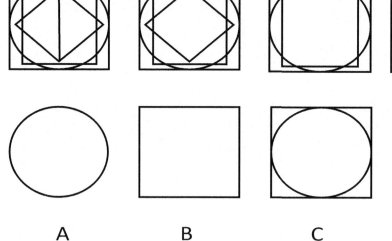

A	B	C	D	E

QUESTION 18

What comes next in the sequence?

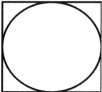

A	B	C	D

QUESTION 19

What comes next in the sequence?

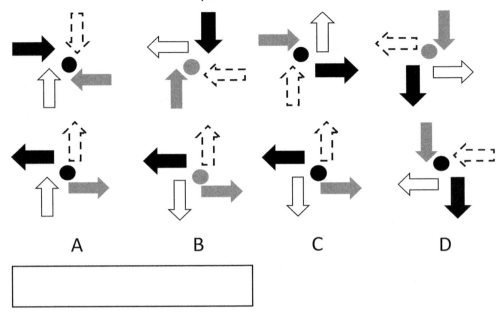

A   B   C   D

QUESTION 20

What comes next in the sequence?

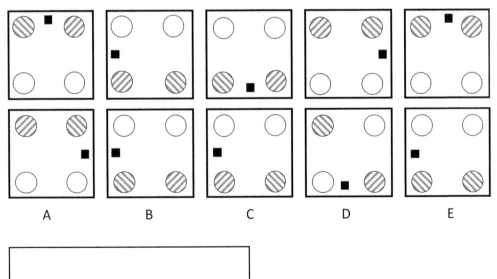

A   B   C   D   E

ANSWERS TO SECTION 3

Q1. E

Rule 1 = each figure must contain a square.

Figure E is the odd one out because all of the other figures contain a square, whereas Figure E does not follow this rule and therefore makes it the odd one out.

Q2. D

Rule 1 = there must be at least one line of symmetry through the figure.

Figure A can be ruled out because it has no lines of symmetry. Figure B can be ruled out because it has no lines of symmetry. Figure C can be ruled out because the black star on the left would not reflect the black star on the right. Figure E can be ruled out because the black square on the left would not reflect the white square on the right.

Q3. E

The rule in this question sees the grey arrows dictating the number of moon shapes in the pattern above. The rule being applied to box with the question mark means that three moon shapes should appear in the answer.

Q4. C

The rule in this question sees the white square dictating the number of arrows pointing to the right in the pattern above. The rule being applied to box with the question mark means that no arrows pointing to the right should appear in the answer.

Q5. D

The rule in this question sees the black plus signs dictating the triangles in the pattern above. The rule being applied to box with the question mark means that three triangles should appear in the answer.

Q6. C

Rule 1 = the centre circle alternates between white and black.

Rule 2 = the circle in the top right corner alternates between black and white. Rule 3 = a line is added through the centre of the circle in a clockwise manner (forming a 'plus-like' shape).

Figure A can be ruled out because the white circle in the top right corner needs to be black. Also, the lines horizontally should be shorter than the lines vertically. Figure B can be ruled out because the black centred circle needs to be white. Figure D can be ruled out because the black centred circle needs to be white. Also, a vertical line and a horizontal line needs to be added (to form a 'plus-like' shape).

Q7. D

Rule 1 = you need to draw the figure without the pen leaving the paper.

Rule 2 = you cannot go over any line more than once.

Figure A can be ruled out because the next line drawn will be a vertical line to form the left side of the house. Figure B can be ruled out because a diagonal line has disappeared and instead has drawn in the rest of the outer house. Figure C can be ruled out because your next figure will still have 2 lines missing. Figure E can be ruled out because you cannot draw both the bottom line of the house and the left vertical line.

Q8. C

Rule 1 = an extra line of symmetry is added as the sequence progresses.

Figure A can be ruled out because this has no lines of symmetry. Figure B can be ruled out because a circle is symmetrical no matter what way you rotate it. Figure D can be ruled out because this shape has 4 lines of symmetry; we need a shape with 6 lines of symmetry. Figure E can be ruled out because this only has 1 line of symmetry.

Q9. A

Rule 1 = the figure is rotated 90° clockwise as the sequence progresses.

Figure B can be ruled out because it has been rotated approximately 90° anti- clockwise. Figure C can be ruled out because this has been rotated less than 90° clockwise. Figure D can be ruled out because this has been less than 90° rotated (anti-clockwise). Figure E can be ruled out because it has been rotated 180°.

Q10. D

Rule 1 = the first shape in each of the figures, must be the same as the last shape in the previous box.

Rule 2 = the shape with the most number of sides is black.

Rule 3 = all the sides of each shape in the figure must add up to 10.

Figure A can be ruled out because the sides only add up to 9. Figure B can be ruled out because the sides only add up to 8. Figure C can be ruled out because the sides only add up to 9. Figure E can be ruled out because the sides add up to 11. Also, the shape with the most sides is a square; however there are two squares in this figure, so both squares should be black.

Q11. C

Rule 1 = the figure rotates 90° clockwise as the sequence progresses.
Rule 2 = as the sequence progresses, the black shape switches sides.

Rule 3 = the shaded shape disappears in the next box; and the shape closest to the middle becomes the shaded shape.

Figure A can be ruled out because the small horizontal rectangle should have disappeared. Figure B can be ruled out because the shaded shape should be the small vertical rectangle, not the small horizontal rectangle. Figure D can be ruled out because the figure has been rotated the wrong way, and the black shape should be the vertical rectangle, not the horizontal rectangle. Figure E can be ruled out because the figure has been rotated the wrong way and the shaded rectangle, should be vertical not horizontal.

Q12. B

Rule 1 = the white shape at the end of the figure, becomes a black figure at the start of the next figure.

Rule 2 = the white shape is also rotated 90° clockwise to form the first shape of the next figure.

Rule 3 = both shapes need to be joined at one of the points of each shape.

Figure A can be ruled out because the black shape has not been rotated 90° clockwise (from the previous figure). Figure C can be ruled out because the trapezoid should be black. Also, the shapes need to be joined at points from both shapes. Figure D can be ruled out because the shapes are not joining by the points of both shapes. Figure E can be ruled out because the shapes are not joining by the points of both shapes.

Q13. D

Rule 1 = each shape needs to contain 2 lines of symmetry.

Figure A can be ruled out because it only has 1 line of symmetry. Figure B can be ruled out because it has no lines of symmetry. Figure C can be ruled out because it has 4 lines of symmetry. Figure E can be ruled out because it has 1 line of symmetry.

Q14. B

The rule in this question sees the double-sided arrow dictating the number of patterned squares in the pattern above. The rule being applied to box with the question mark means that two patterned squares should appear in the answer.

Q15. B

Rule 1 = the shapes move round one place clockwise in each figure.

Figure A can be ruled out because the two squares are in the wrong place; the black square should be where the white square is; and the white square should be where the black square is. Figure C can be ruled out because this is a horizontal reflection of answer option A. Figure D can be ruled out because this is a vertical reflection of answer option C.

Q16. E

Rule 1 = the five pointed stars moves around all the points of the cross, two spaces clockwise.

Rule 2 = the four pointed stars moves around all the points of the cross, one space anti-clockwise.

Rule 3 = if two or more stars interlink at the same point, the stars become a grey shape.

Figure A can be ruled out because the stars are in the incorrect position. Figure B can be ruled out because it is a replica of box 2. Figure C can be ruled out because none of the stars should overlap at the points. Figure D can be ruled out because the stars are in the incorrect position.

Q17. A

Rule 1 = starting from the top of the figure, and moving around the outer edge of the shape, in a clockwise motion, one square is removed each time.

Figure B can be ruled out because we would be left with four squares. Figure C can be ruled out because the four squares should form a cross-like shape. Figure D can be ruled out because the four squares should form a cross- like shape. Figure E can be ruled out because the shape should have four squares, not three.

Q18. B

Rule 1 = working from the inside of the shape, outwards, one shape disappears each time.

Figure A can be ruled out because the shape on the outside is a square; and therefore a square would remain. Figure C can be ruled out because this is a replica of box 4. Figure D can be ruled out because one of the answers is correct; so therefore it cannot be 'none'.

Q19. C

Rule 1 = the figure rotates 90° clockwise as the sequence progresses.

Rule 2 = the dot in the centre alternates from black to grey, as the sequence progresses.

Rule 3 = the arrows begin all pointing inwards. As the sequence progresses, one arrow is turned outwards.

Figure A can be ruled out because the white arrow is pointing inwards; all the arrows should be pointing outwards. Figure B can be ruled out because the grey dot should be a black dot. Figure D can be ruled out because the dashed arrow should be pointing outwards as opposed to inwards.

Q20. C

Rule 1 = the black square rotates 90° anti-clockwise.

Rule 2 = the downward hatching circle follows the pattern of: top left, bottom right, bottom left, top right. The sequence then repeats.

Rule 3 = the upward hatching circle follows the pattern of: top right, bottom left, bottom right, top left. The sequence then repeats.

INDUCTIVE REASONING
SECTION 4

QUESTION 1

Which figure is the odd one out?

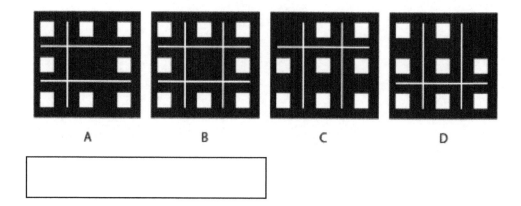

A   B   C   D

QUESTION 2

Which figure is the odd one out?

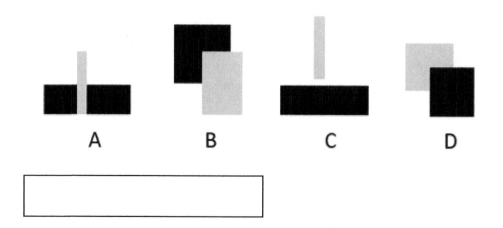

A   B   C   D

QUESTION 3

What comes next in the sequence?

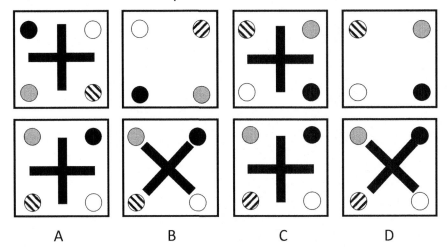

| A | B | C | D |

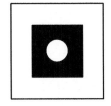  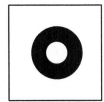 

| A | B | C | D |

 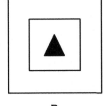  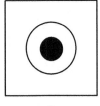

QUESTION 4

Fill in the missing gap in order to complete the sequence.

QUESTION 5

Fill in the missing gap in order to complete the sequence.

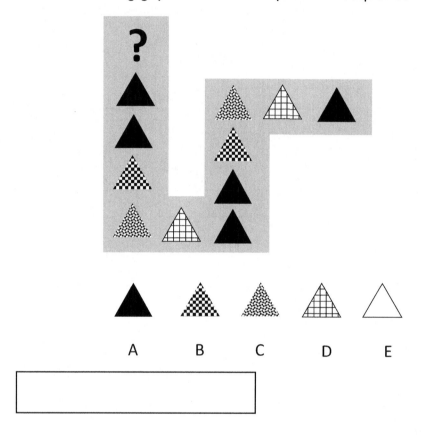

A	B	C	D	E

QUESTION 6

Which figure is the odd one out?

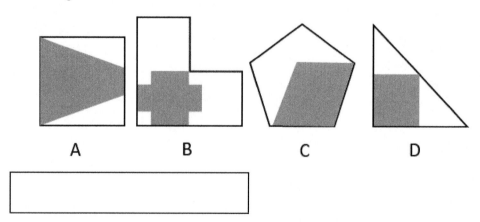

A	B	C	D

QUESTION 7

Fill in the missing gap in order to complete the sequence.

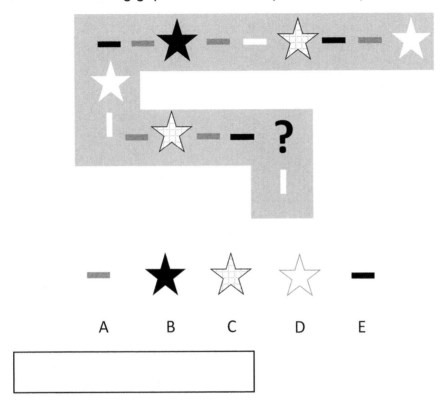

A   B   C   D   E

QUESTION 8

Which figure is the odd one out?

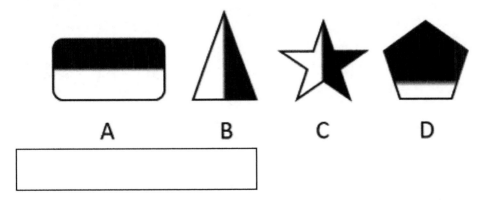

A   B   C   D

QUESTION 9

Fill in the missing gap in order to complete the sequence.

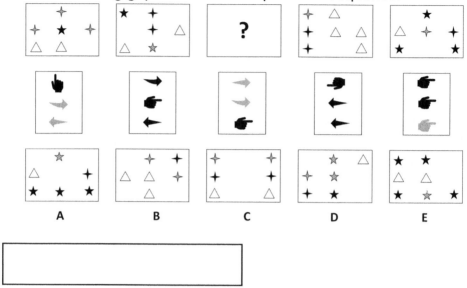

QUESTION 10

Fill in the missing gap in order to complete the sequence.

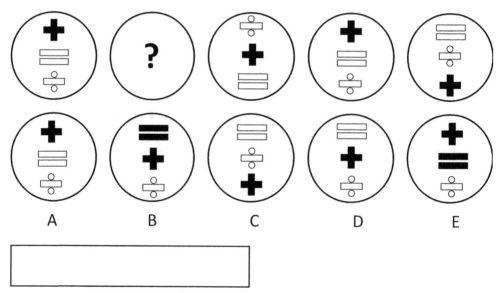

QUESTION 11

Fill in the missing gap in order to complete the sequence.

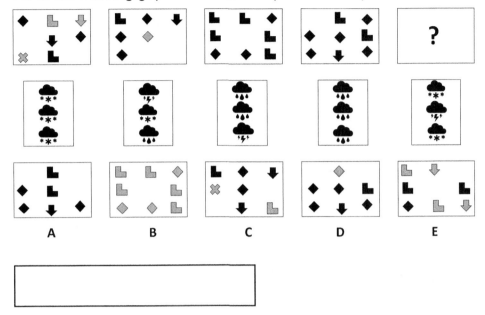

QUESTION 12

Which figure comes next in the sequence?

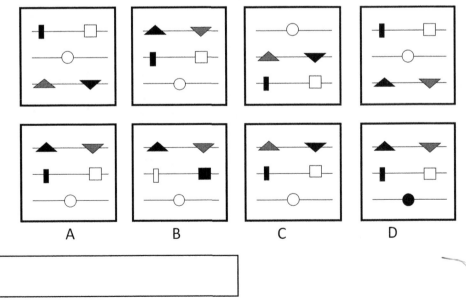

QUESTION 13

What comes next in the sequence?

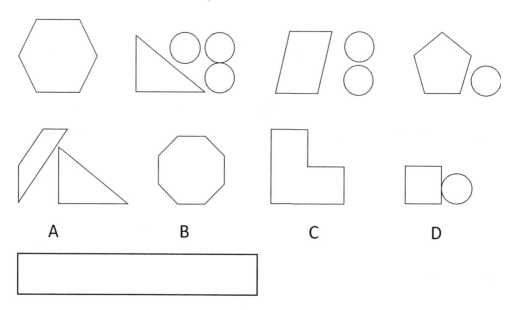

A	B	C	D

QUESTION 14

Fill in the gap in order to complete the sequence.

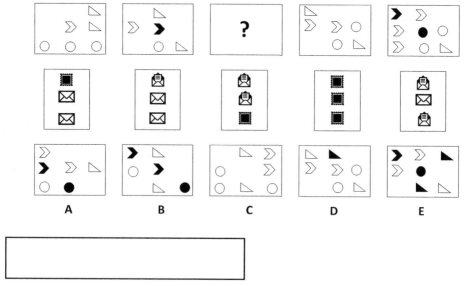

QUESTION 15

Fill in the missing gap in order to complete the sequence.

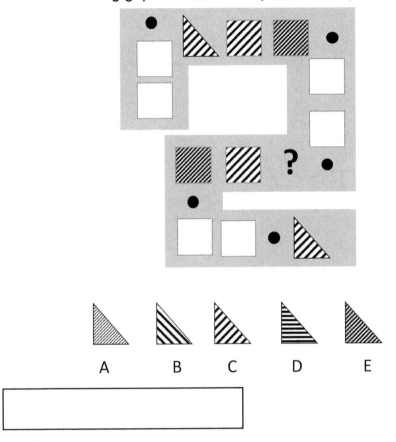

A   B   C   D   E

QUESTION 16

Which figure is the odd one out?

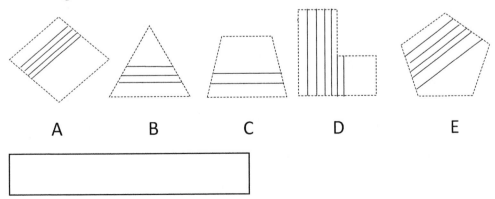

A   B   C   D   E

QUESTION 17

Fill in the missing gap in order to complete the sequence.

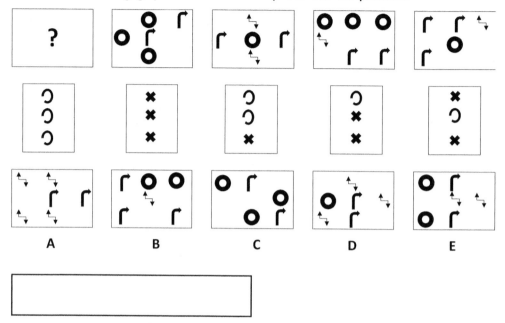

QUESTION 18

Which figure fits in with the sequence?

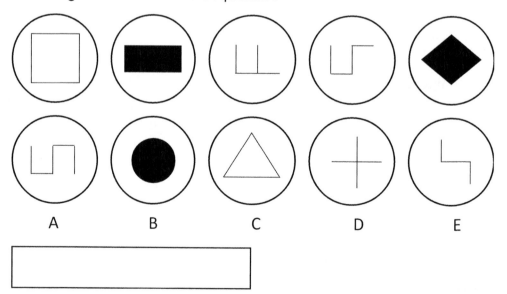

QUESTION 19

Fill in the missing gap in order to complete the sequence.

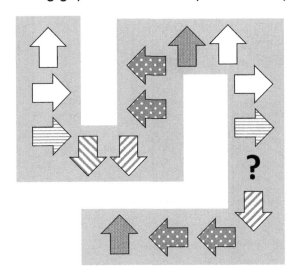

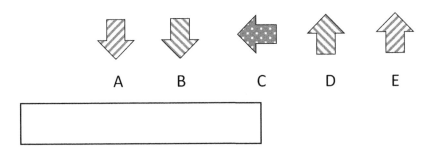

A   B   C   D   E

QUESTION 20

What comes next in the sequence?

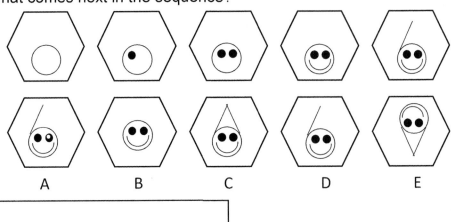

A   B   C   D   E

QUESTION 21

What comes next in the sequence?

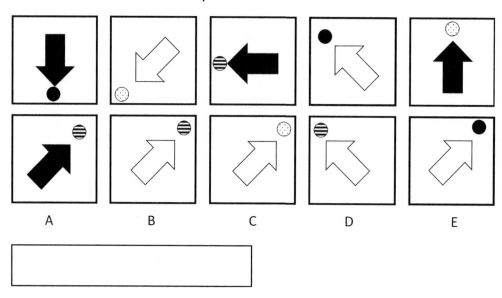

A   B   C   D   E

QUESTION 22

Fill in the missing gap in order to complete the sequence.

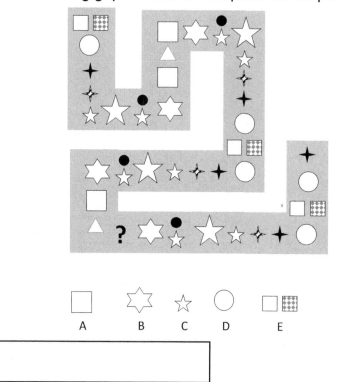

A   B   C   D   E

QUESTION 23

Which figure fits in with the sequence?

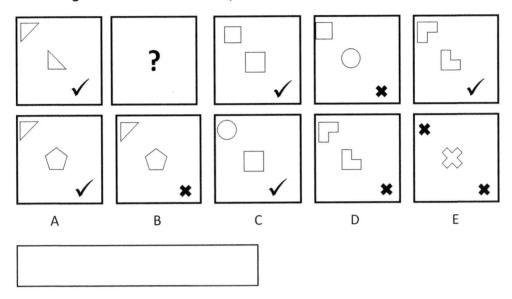

QUESTION 24

What comes next in the sequence?

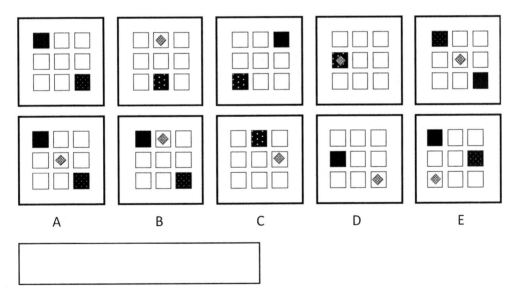

QUESTION 25

What comes next in the sequence?

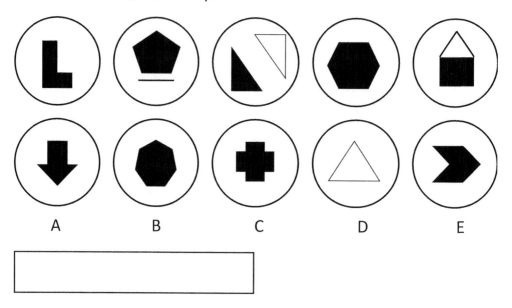

| A | B | C | D | E |

QUESTION 26

Which figure is the odd one out?

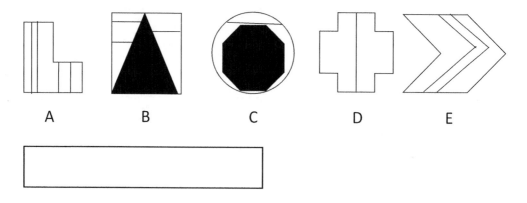

| A | B | C | D | E |

QUESTION 27

Fill in the missing gap in order to complete the sequence.

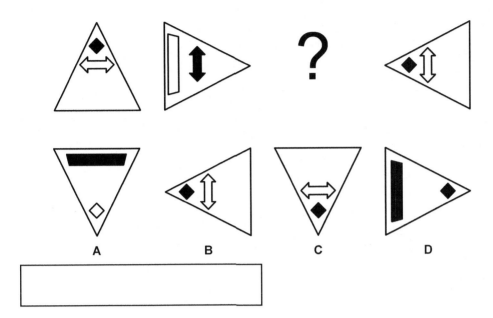

QUESTION 28

Fill in the missing gap in order to complete the sequence.

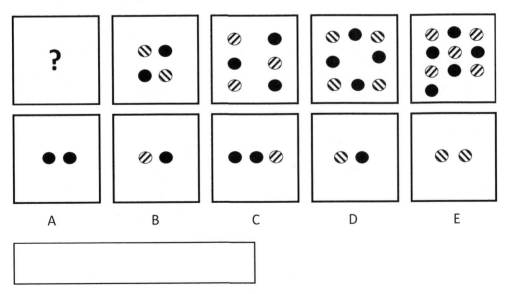

QUESTION 29

What comes next in the sequence?

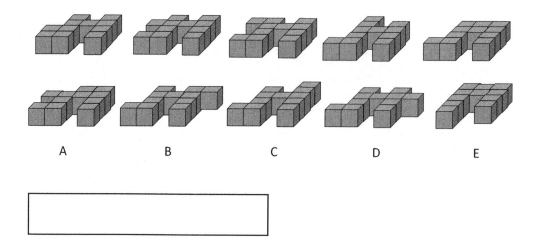

A   B   C   D   E

QUESTION 30

What comes next in the sequence?

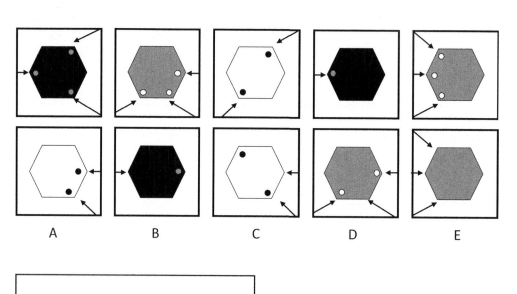

A   B   C   D   E

QUESTION 31

Fill in the missing gap in order to complete the sequence.

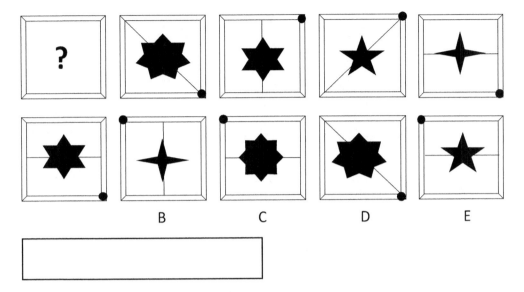

B   C   D   E

QUESTION 32

Fill in the missing gap in order to complete the sequence.

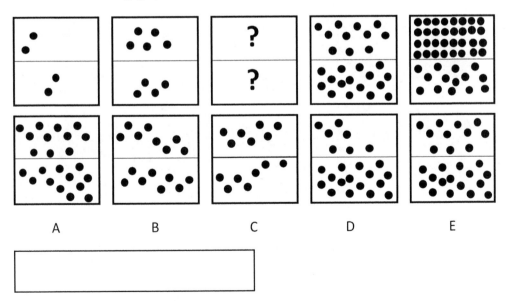

A   B   C   D   E

QUESTION 33

What comes next in the sequence?

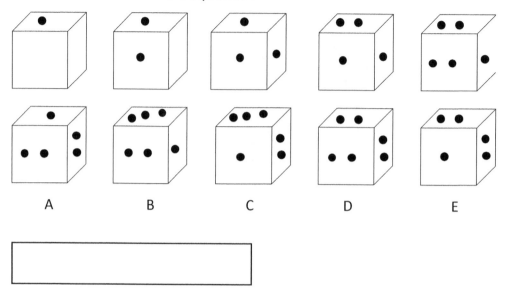

| A | B | C | D | E |

QUESTION 34

Fill in the missing gap in order to complete the sequence.

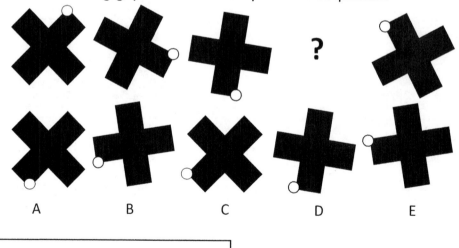

| A | B | C | D | E |

QUESTION 35

Fill in the missing gap in order to complete the sequence.

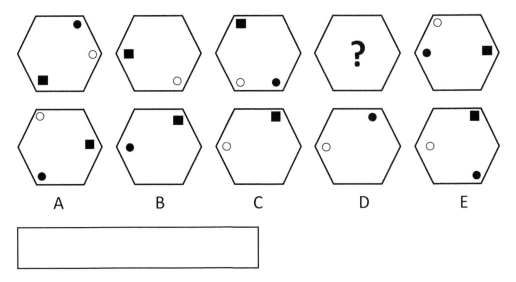

A   B   C   D   E

QUESTION 36

Fill in the missing gap in order to complete the sequence.

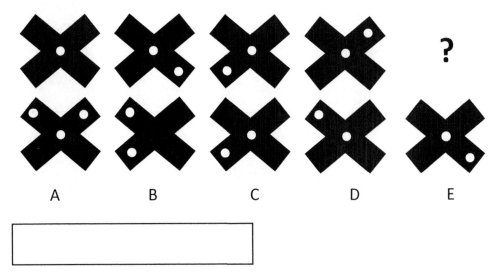

A   B   C   D   E

QUESTION 37

What comes next in the sequence?

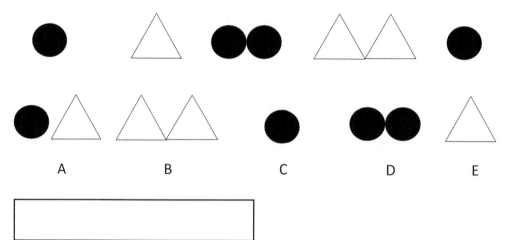

A   B   C   D   E

QUESTION 38

Fill in the missing gap in order to complete the sequence.

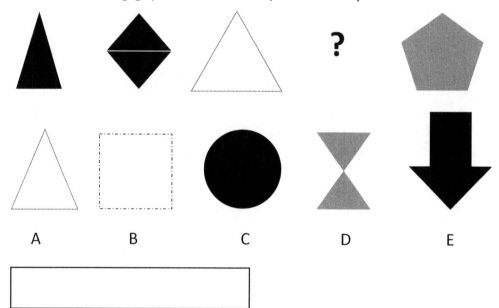

A   B   C   D   E

QUESTION 39

Which figure comes next in the sequence?

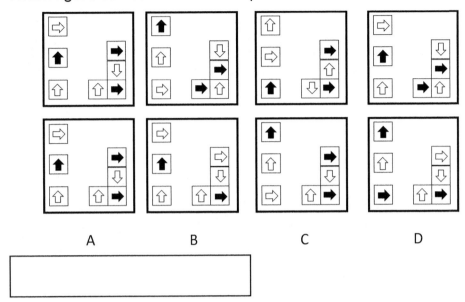

A   B   C   D

QUESTION 40

Fill in the missing gap in order to complete the sequence.

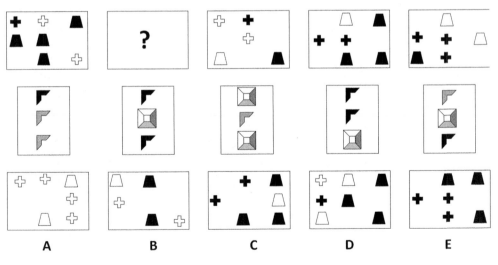

A   B   C   D   E

ANSWERS TO SECTION 4

Q1. B

Figure B is the odd one out because all of the other figures contain three lines, whereas Figure B contains four lines.

Q2. C

Figure C is the odd one out because all of the other figures contain two shapes that overlap; whereas Figure C has two shapes but are not overlapping.

Q3. C

The sequence alternates from a black plus sign to a black cross sign. The circles move around the square one corner anti-clockwise.

Q4. B

Rule 1 = the large shape alternates from black to white.

Rule 2 = the large shapes follow the pattern of: square, triangle, circle and so forth.

Rule 3 = the small shapes alternate from white to black.

Rule 4 = the small shapes alternate between circles and triangles.

Figure A can be ruled out because we need a triangle inside a square; not a square inside a triangle. Figure C can be ruled out because we need a triangle inside a square. Figure D can be ruled out because we need a triangle inside a square.

Q5. D

If you look carefully at the whole sequence, you will notice that Figure D always comes before the two black triangles. Therefore, the correct answer is D.

Q6. B

Figure B is the odd one out because the shaded shape should contain four sides. All of the other figures contain a shaded shape with four sides; whereas Figure B contains a shaded shape of twelve sides and therefore makes it the odd one out.

Q7. B

If you look carefully at the whole sequence, you will notice that the stars follow the colour pattern of: white, patterned, black, which is then repeated. The sequence is missing a black star; and we know this because a patterned star was the last star in the sequence and a black star should follow.

Q8. D

Figure D is the odd one out because all of the other figures are shaded exactly half; whereas Figure D is shaded more than half.

Q9. D

The rule in this question sees the number of shapes pointing to the right dictating the number of star shapes in the pattern above. The rule being applied to box with the question mark means that three star shapes should appear in the answer.

Q10. C

Rule 1 = the shapes move up the sequence one place at a time.

Figure A can be ruled out because all the shapes need to move up another place. Figure B can be ruled out because the plus sign and the divide sign should be in each other's place. Also, the equals sign should be white, not black. Figure D can be ruled out because the plus sign and the divide sign are in the wrong place. Figure E can be ruled out because all the shapes are in the incorrect position. Also, the equals sign should be white, not black.

Q11. C

The rule in this question sees the number of snow clouds dictating the number of grey shapes in the pattern above. The rule being applied to box with the question mark means that two grey shapes should appear in the answer.

Q12. C

Rule 1 = the shapes move down one line as the sequence progresses.

Rule 2 = once they reach the bottom, they go back to the top.

Rule 3 = the two triangles alternate colours from black to grey and vice versa.

Figure A can be ruled out because the black triangle should be grey; and the grey triangle should be black. Figure B can be ruled out because the black triangle should be grey; and the grey triangle should be black. Also, the thin rectangle should be black; and the square should be white. Figure D can be ruled out because the black triangle should be grey; and the grey triangle should be black. Also, the black circle should be white.

Q13. C

Rule 1 = all the figures must contain shapes with sides that all add up to 6.

Figure A can be ruled out because all the sides add up to 7. Figure B can be ruled out because all the sides add up to 8. Figure D can be ruled out because all the sides only add up to 5.

Q14. A

The rule in this question sees the number of open envelopes dictating the number of black shapes in the pattern above. The rule being applied to box with the question mark means that two black shapes should appear in the answer.

Q15. C

If you look carefully at the whole sequence, you will notice a recurring pattern. The triangle does not change pattern; it stays the same throughout. Therefore, you need the same pattern as the triangles already show. The correct answer is C, because C has diagonal lines from top left to bottom right.

Q16. C

Figure C is the odd one out because all of the other figures have the same amount of lines inside the shape as the shape's number of sides. For example, a triangle has three sides, therefore there are three lines drawn inside the shape. Figure C is a four sided shape and only has two lines drawn in the shape; and therefore makes it the odd one out.

Q17. D

The rule in this question sees the number of horseshoe shapes dictating the number of double-sided arrows in the pattern above. The rule being applied to box with the question mark means that three double-sided arrows should appear in the answer.

Q18. D

Rule 1 = each figure must contain 4 sides.

Figure A can be ruled out because the shape contains 5 sides. Figure B can be ruled out because a circle has 1 continuous side. Figure C can be ruled out because the shape only contains 3 sides. Figure E can be ruled out because the shape only contains 3 sides.

Q19. B

The next arrow after the shaded horizontal arrow (facing towards the right), would be a downward pointing arrow; with diagonal lines going from top left to bottom right.

Q20. C

Rule 1 = you are adding one shape to the previous figure in order to complete the overall shape.

Figure A can be ruled out because a line should be added to finish the figures hat; there should not be a white circle in the middle of the eye. Figure B can be ruled out because this has gone back a previous step. Figure D can be ruled out because this is an exact replica of box 5. Figure E can be ruled out because the figure should not have been rotated; none of the other figures in the sequence have been rotated, therefore the next figure in the sequence should also not be rotated.

Q21. B

Rule 1 = the arrow moves 45° clockwise.

Rule 2 = the arrow alternates colour from black to white, as the sequence progresses.

Rule 3 = the dot is placed underneath the point of the arrow.

Rule 4 = the dot alternates colour and changes from: black, dotted, to striped. The sequence repeats.

Figure A can be ruled out because the arrow needs to be white, not black. Figure C can be ruled out because the dotted line needs to have horizontal stripes. Figure D can be ruled out because the arrow should be pointing to the top right corner, not the top left. Also, the dot needs to be in the top right corner. Figure E can be ruled out because the black dot needs to be horizontal stripes.

Q22. A

If you look closely at the sequence, you will notice that there are 10 figures which are repeated throughout the sequence. The sequence then uses these 10 figures and works backwards. For example, imagine the figures were numbers; it would look something like this: 1, 2, 3, 4, 5, 6, 7, 8, 9, 10, 9, 8, 7, 6, 5 and so forth. Therefore, the figure that we need in order to replace the question mark is, a white square.

Q23. B

Rule 1 = if the shape in the middle of the square is the same as the shape in the top left corner, then the shape in the bottom right corner is a 'tick'.

Rule 2 = if the shape in the middle of the square is not the same as the shape in the top left corner, then the shape in the bottom right corner is a 'cross'.

Figure A can be ruled out because the shape in the middle is not the same as the shape in the top left corner; so therefore the figure cannot contain a tick (it should be a cross instead). Figure C can be ruled out because the shape in the middle is not the same as the shape in the top left corner; so therefore the figure cannot contain a tick (it should be a cross instead). Figure D can be ruled out because the shape in the middle is the same as the shape in the top left corner; so therefore the figure should contain a tick, not a cross. Figure E can be ruled out because the pattern does not follow the same patterned sequence as the previous figures.

Q24. C

Rule 1 = the black square moves around the outer edge in an anti-clockwise motion. It moves three spaces as the sequence progresses.

Rule 2 = the black patterned square moves one space clockwise around the outer edge.

Rule 3 = the diamond shape moves one space from left to right, once it reaches the end, it starts back at the left on the next row.

Rule 4 = if the black square and black patterned square end in the same square, the square becomes black and patterned.

Figure A can be ruled out because the black square and the black patterned square should both be on the top row in the middle. The diamond shape should be on the middle row to the right. Figure B can be ruled because the black square and the black patterned square should both be on the top row in the middle. The diamond shape should be on the middle row, to the right. Figure D can be ruled out because the black square should be combined with the patterned square and form the middle square on the top row. The diamond shape should be on the middle row, to the right. Figure E can be ruled out because the black square and the black patterned square should both be on the top row in the middle. The diamond shape should be on the middle row to the right.

Q25. E

Rule 1 = each figure must contain 6 sides.

Figure A can be ruled out because the shape contains 7 sides. Figure B can be ruled out because the shape contains 7 sides. Figure C can be ruled out because the shape contains 12 sides. Figure D can be ruled out because the shape contains 3 sides.

Q26. D

Figure D is the odd one out because all of the other figures contain shapes in which the sides all add up to 10. For example, in Figure A, it contains an 'L' shape (which contains 6 sides); the 'L' shape contain 4 horizontal lines; so therefore the sides all add up to 10.

Q27. A

Rule 1 = the triangle is being rotated 90° clockwise as the sequence progresses.

Rule 2 = the shapes inside the triangle remain in the same position; however the colour pattern changes. The colour pattern moves down one each time, and once it reaches the bottom, it goes back to the top.

Q28. B

Rule 1 = the number of dots increase by 2 each time.

Rule 2 = the diagonal lines alternate from top left to bottom right; to top right to bottom left.

Rule 3 = the number of black dots increases by 1 each time.

Figure A can be ruled out because the first figure should contain one black dot and one striped dot. Figure C can be ruled out because the first figure should contain only two dots, not three. Figure D can be ruled out because the diagonal lines are pointing the wrong way; they should be top right to bottom left; not top left to bottom right. Figure E can be ruled out because there should be one black dot and one striped dot.

Q29. C

Rule 1 = the first square in the first column moves around the outer edge of the shape one space in a clockwise motion.

Figures A, B, D and E can all be ruled out because the square that is rotating around the outer edge is in the incorrect position for each figure, apart from Figure C.

Q30. A

Rule 1 = the hexagon alternates colour. It changes colour from black, grey, white, black, grey, white and so forth.

Rule 2 = the black arrows must be touching the outer squared box.

Rule 3 = the black arrows are used to indicate where the circles should be inside the hexagon.

Rule 4 = the circles inside the shapes follow the colour pattern of: grey, white, black, grey, white, black and so forth.

Figure B can be ruled out because the arrow on the left side of the square, in the middle, should have a circle directly next to it (inside the hexagon); instead the circle is in the middle right corner of the hexagon. Figure C can be ruled out because the circle in the top left corner of the hexagon should be positioned in the middle right corner of the hexagon. Figure D can be ruled out because the middle arrow is pointing to an empty space; either the arrow should be removed or a circle placed where the arrow is pointing. Figure E can be ruled out because there are three arrows, and no circles; the arrows are used to illustrate where the circles are to be positioned.

Q31. C

Rule 1 = the black star-shape in the middle of the figure loses one point as the sequence progresses. For example, a six-sided star becomes a five-sided star and then a four-sided star and so on.

Rule 2 = the black dot on the corner of the square rotates clockwise one place, then two places, then three, then four. Once it reaches four it works backwards (anticlockwise): three spaces, then two, then one and so forth.

Rule 3 = the line in the middle of the shape rotates 45° clockwise, as the sequence progresses.

Figure A can be ruled out because the black star needs to have eight points. Also, the black dot should be in the top left corner. Figure B can be ruled out because the black star needs to have eight points, not four. Also, the vertical line should be horizontal. Figure D can be ruled out because the black star needs to have eight points, not seven. Also, the diagonal line should be horizontal and the black dot should be in the top left corner. Figure E can be ruled out because the five-sided star should be an eight-sided star.

Q32. B

Rule 1 = working from the first figure (in the top half of the box), and using a zig-zag method throughout the sequence, it follows the pattern of: doubling each time (2, 4, 8, 16 and 32).

Rule 2 = working from the first figure (in the bottom half of the box), and using a zig-zag method throughout the sequence, it follows the pattern of: adding three dots each time (2, 5, 8, 11 and 14).

Figure's A, C, D and E can all be ruled out because the top half of the box needs to contain eight dots, and the bottom half of the box needs to contain eight dots.

Q33. D

Rule 1 = one dot is added each time, as the sequence progresses.

Rule 2 = the dots are added on each face of the cube in the following order: top, left, right, top, left, right and so forth.

Figure A can be ruled out because there should be six dots on the 6th figure. There should be another dot added to the top face of the cube.

Figure B can be ruled out because there should only be two dots on the top face; two dots should be positioned on the right side of the cube. Figure C can be ruled out because there should only be two dots on the top face of the cube; two dots should be positioned on the left side of the cube. Figure E can be ruled out because there should be six dots on the 6th figure; another dot should be placed on the left face of the cube.

Q34. B

Rule 1 = there are 5 figures and the rotations have been equally divided amongst all of the figures. So, $360° ÷ 5 = 72°$. So, the figures are being rotated 72° clockwise.

Figure A can be ruled out because this has been rotated less than 72° from the previous figure. Figure C can be ruled out because the white dot is on the wrong corner of the cross sign; the dot should be moved down one point; and the whole figure needs to be rotated exactly 72°. Figure D can be ruled out because the cross sign has not been rotated from the previous figure (it is the same); the dot has been moved one space above where it should be. Figure E can be ruled out because the white dot is in the incorrect position; it should be moved down one point.

Q35. C

Rule 1 = the black square rotates around the hexagon one space clockwise.

Rule 2 = the black circle rotates around the hexagon two spaces anti- clockwise.

Rule 3 = the white circle rotates around the hexagon one space clockwise.

Rule 4 = if any of the shapes end up in the same place, it automatically becomes a black square.

Figure A can be ruled out because the black square should be in the top right corner, and the white circle should be in the middle left corner; the black dot should have disappeared behind the black square. Figure B can be ruled out because the black dot should be a white dot instead. Figure D can be ruled out because the black dot should have automatically changed to a black square (the black square and the black dot ended up in the same position). Figure E can be ruled out because the black dot in the bottom right corner should not be there; it should have disappeared behind the black square.

Q36. D

Rule 1 = the white dot in the middle of the cross stays in the same position throughout the sequence.

Rule 2 = the white dot starting in the bottom right corner follows the following pattern: bottom right, bottom left, top right, top left.

Figure A can be ruled out because there should only be two dots in the figure, not three; the white dot in the top right corner should be removed. Figure B can be ruled out because there should be a white dot in the middle of the cross; the dot in the bottom left corner should be positioned in the centre of the cross. Figure C can be ruled out because the white dot in the bottom left corner should be in the top left corner. Figure E can be ruled out because the white dot in the bottom right corner should be positioned in the top left corner.

Q37. E

Rule 1 = the sequence repeats itself after the 4th figure.

Figures A, B, C and D can all be ruled out because the next figure should be a single white triangle.

Q38. B

Rule 1 = a line of symmetry is added each time. For example, the isosceles triangle has 1 line of symmetry, the diamond shape has two lines of symmetry and so forth.

Figure A can be ruled out because the shape only has one line of symmetry, Figure C can be ruled out because a circle is symmetrical no matter what way you rotate it. Figure D can be ruled out because the shape has two lines of symmetry. Figure E can be ruled out because the shape only has one line of symmetry.

Q39. C

Rule 1 = the 3 squares to the left move up one space each time as the sequence progresses.

Rule 2 = the 4 shapes to the right move up one space each time as the sequence progresses.

Figures A, B and D can all be ruled out because the shapes are in the incorrect position.

Q40. C

The rule in this question sees the number of grey shapes dictating the number of white shapes in the pattern above. The rule being applied to box with the question mark means that one white shape should appear in the answer.

INDUCTIVE REASONING
SECTION 5

QUESTION 1

What comes next in the sequence?

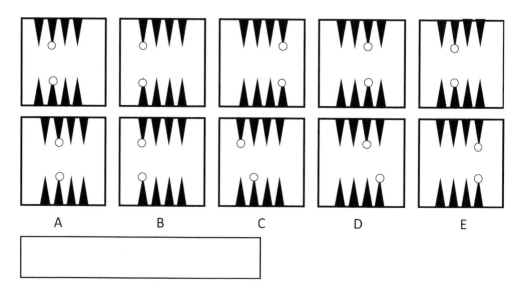

QUESTION 2

Fill in the missing gap in order to complete the sequence.

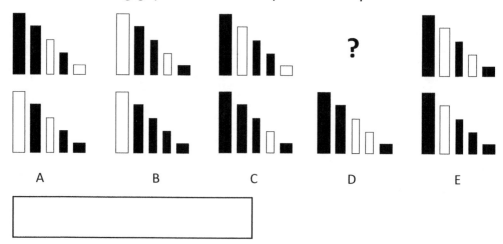

QUESTION 3

What comes next in the sequence?

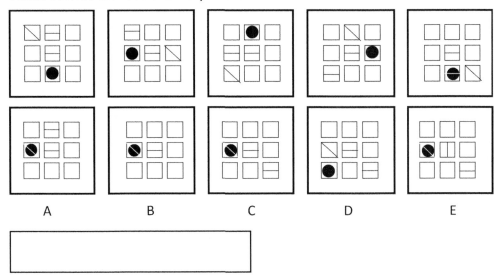

A   B   C   D   E

QUESTION 4

Fill in the missing gap in order to complete the sequence.

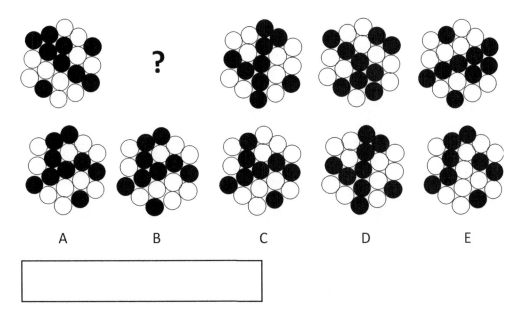

A   B   C   D   E

QUESTION 5

Which figure is the odd one out?

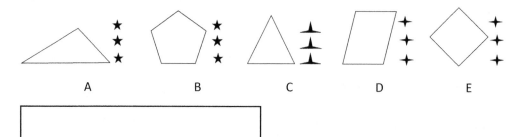

| A | B | C | D | E |

QUESTION 6

Which figure is the odd one out?

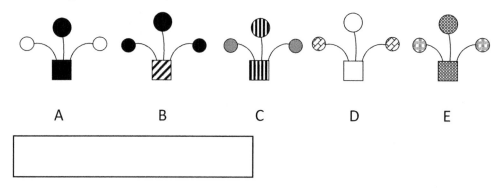

| A | B | C | D | E |

QUESTION 7

Which figure is the odd one out?

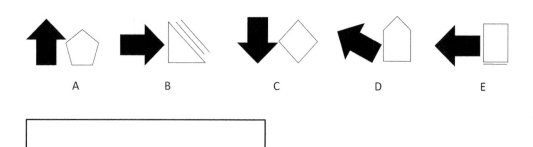

| A | B | C | D | E |

QUESTION 8

Fill in the gap in order to complete the sequence.

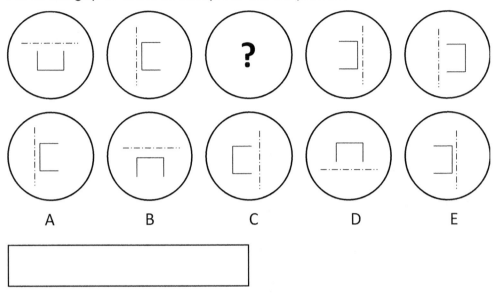

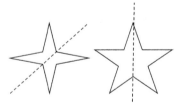

QUESTION 9

Which Answer Figure fits in with the two Question Figures?

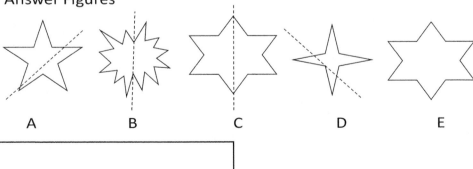

QUESTION 10

Which Answer Figure fits in with the two Question Figures?

Question Figures

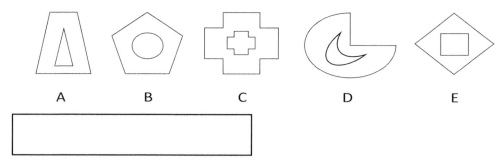

Answer Figures

A   B   C   D   E

QUESTION 11

Which figure is the odd one out?

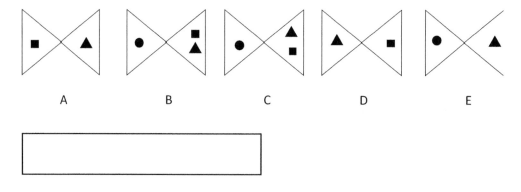

A   B   C   D   E

QUESTION 12

Which Answer Figure fits in with the two Question Figures?

Question Figures

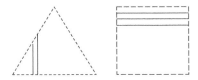

Answer Figures

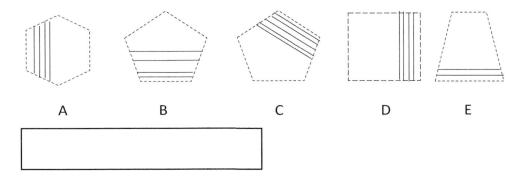

| A | B | C | D | E |

QUESTION 13

Fill in the gap in order to complete the sequence.

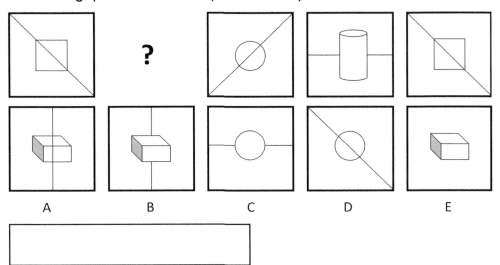

| A | B | C | D | E |

QUESTION 14

What comes next in the sequence?

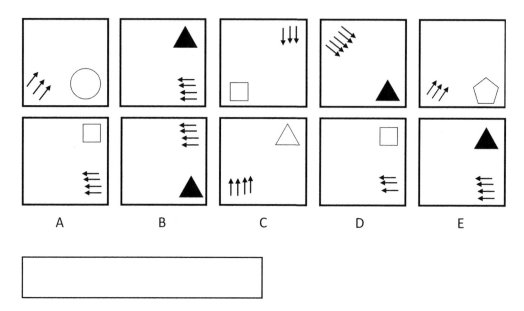

A   B   C   D   E

QUESTION 15

What comes next in the sequence?

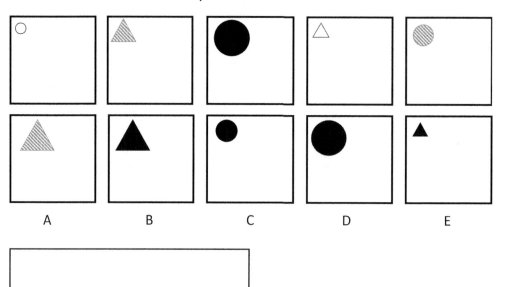

A   B   C   D   E

QUESTION 16

Which Answer Figure fits in with the two Question Figures?

Question Figures

Answer Figures

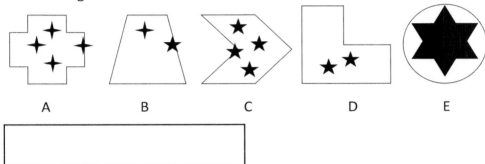

| A | B | C | D | E |

QUESTION 17

Which figure is the odd one out?

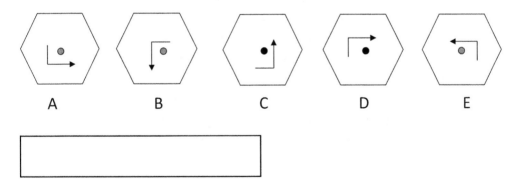

| A | B | C | D | E |

QUESTION 18

Which figure is the odd one out?

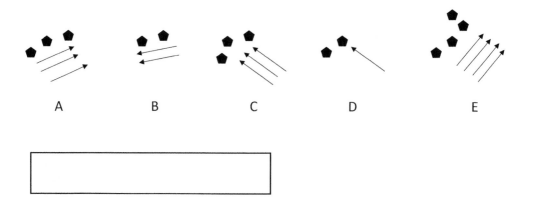

A   B   C   D   E

QUESTION 19

Fill in the gap in order to complete the sequence.

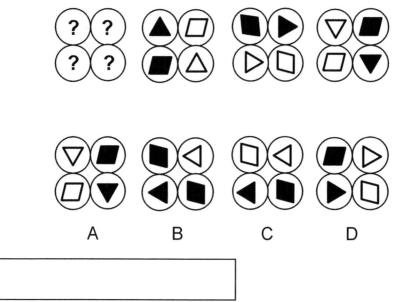

A   B   C   D

QUESTION 20

Which of the Answer Figures fits in with the three Question Figures?

Question Figures

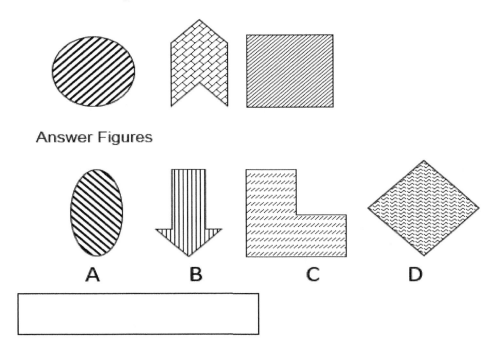

Answer Figures

A   B   C   D

QUESTION 21

Fill in the gap in order to complete the sequence.

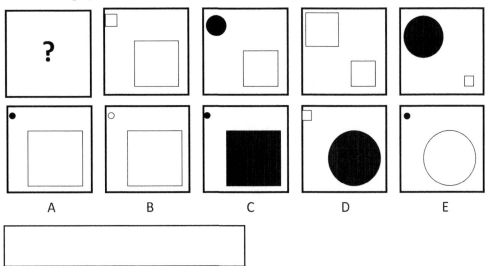

A   B   C   D   E

QUESTION 22

Fill in the gap in order to complete the sequence.

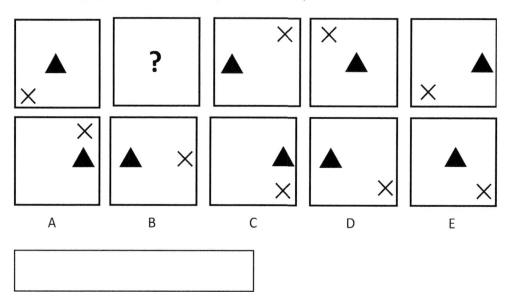

A   B   C   D   E

QUESTION 23

Which figure is the odd one out?

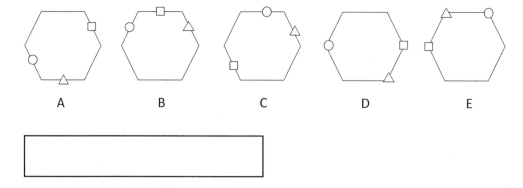

A   B   C   D   E

QUESTION 24

Fill in the gap in order to complete the sequence.

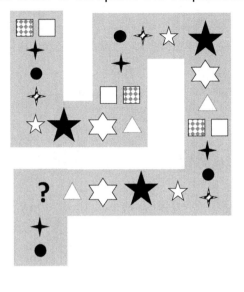

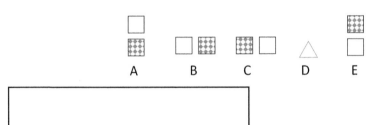

A   B   C   D   E

QUESTION 25

Fill in the gap in order to complete the sequence.

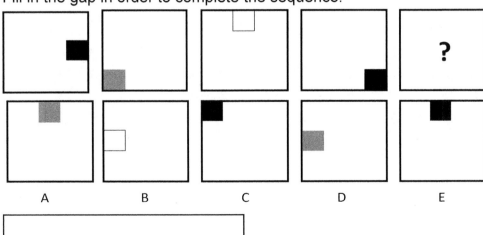

A   B   C   D   E

QUESTION 26

What comes next in the sequence?

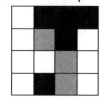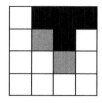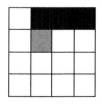

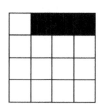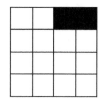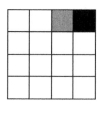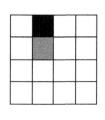

A	B	C	D

QUESTION 27

What comes next in the sequence?

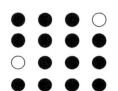

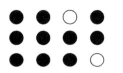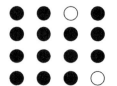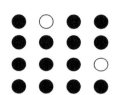

A	B	C	D

QUESTION 28

Fill in the gap in order to complete the sequence.

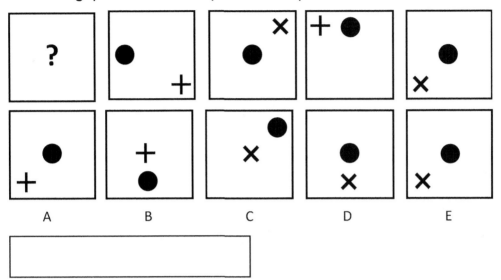

QUESTION 29

Which figure fits in with the sequence?

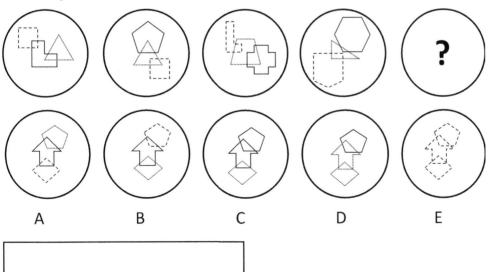

QUESTION 30

What comes next in the sequence?

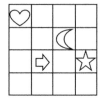 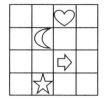 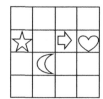 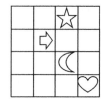

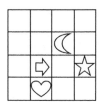 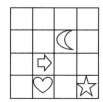 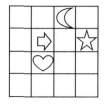 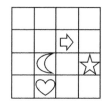

A	B	C	D

QUESTION 31

Which figure is the odd one out?

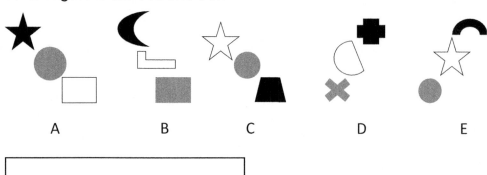

A	B	C	D	E

QUESTION 32

Which Answer Figure fits in with the two Question Figures?

Question Figures

Answer Figures

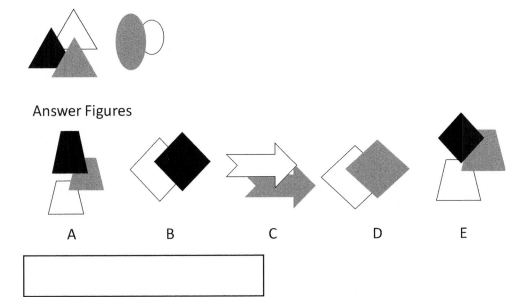

A   B   C   D   E

QUESTION 33

Work out which of the cubes can be made from the cube net.

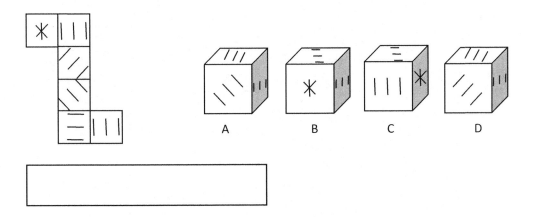

A   B   C   D

QUESTION 34

Which figure is the odd one out?

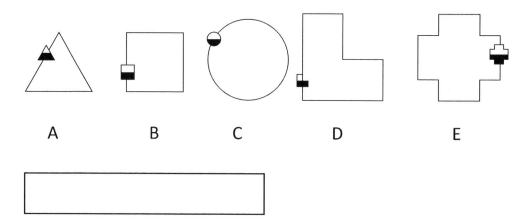

| A | B | C | D | E |

QUESTION 35

Which answer shape is the next one in the series?

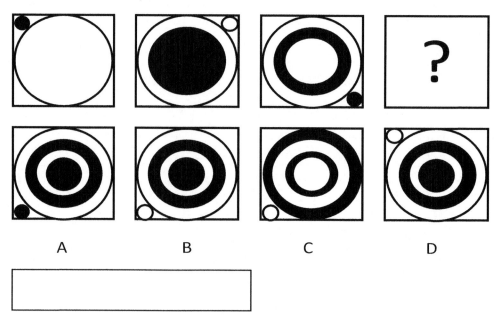

| A | B | C | D |

QUESTION 36

Which figure is the odd one out?

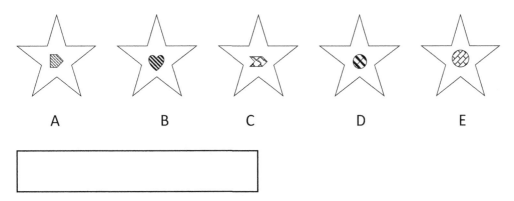

| A | B | C | D | E |

QUESTION 37

Which answer shape is a rotation of the example shape?

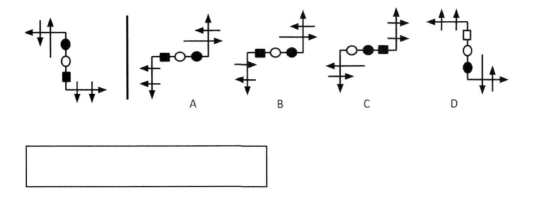

QUESTION 38

What figure comes next in the sequence?

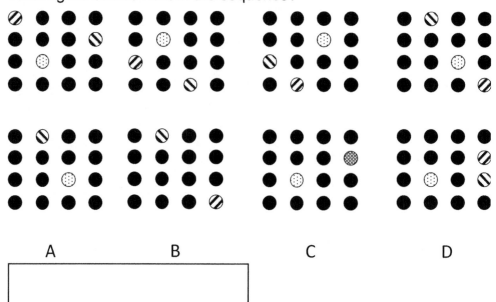

A	B	C	D

QUESTION 39

Which Answer Figure fits in with the two Question Figures?

Question Figures

Answer Figures

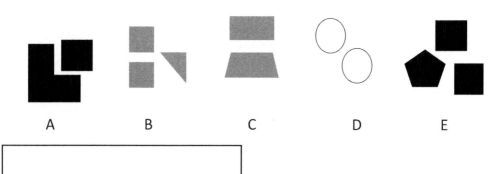

A	B	C	D	E

QUESTION 40

Which figure is the odd one out?

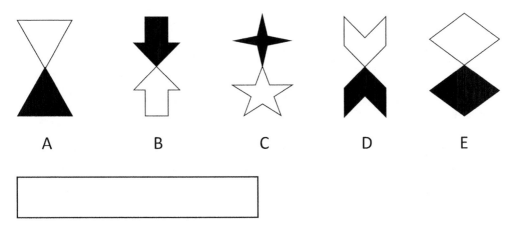

A   B   C   D   E

ANSWERS TO SECTION 5

Q1. B

Rule 1 = on the top row, the circles move one space to the left, once it reaches the end it starts back to the beginning.

Rule 2 = on the bottom row, the circles move one space to the left, once it reaches the end it goes back to the beginning.

Figure A can be ruled out because the circle on the top row needs to be on the first triangle, and the circle on the bottom row also needs to be on the first triangle. Figure C can be ruled out because the circle on the bottom row needs to be on the first triangle. Figure D can be ruled out because the circle on the top row needs to be on the first triangle, and the circle on the bottom row also needs to be on the first triangle. Figure E can be ruled out because both circles need to be on the first triangles of the top and bottom row.

Q2. A

Rule 1 = the colour pattern follows: black, black, white, black and white. This pattern moves down one space each time, as the sequence progresses.

Figure B can be ruled out because there should be three black squares and two white squares, not four black squares and one white square. Figure C can be ruled out because there should be three black squares and two white squares, not four black squares and one white square. Figure D can be ruled out because the colour sequence in this figure should be: white, black, white, black and black. Figure E can be ruled out because the colour pattern should be: white, black, white, black and black.

Q3. C

Rule 1 = the horizontal line in the middle square, stays the same throughout.

Rule 2 = the diagonal line moves around the outer edge three spaces clockwise.

Rule 3 = the horizontal line (around the edge) moves one place anti-clockwise as the sequence progresses.

Rule 4 = the black circle moves around the outer edge two spaces clockwise.

Rule 5 = if a circle interlinks with a line, that line becomes white and is placed within the box and the circle.

Figure A can be ruled out because the horizontal line, around the outer edge, should be on the last row, in the last box. Figure B can be ruled out because a horizontal line is missing; it should be placed on the last row, in the last box. Figure D can be ruled out because the circle should be interlinked with the box that contains the diagonal line; this diagonal line should then become white. Figure E can be ruled out because the box in the middle of the figure should contain a horizontal line, not a vertical line.

Q4. A

Rule 1 = the dot in the centre, remains black throughout the sequence.

Rule 2 = the inner circles (minus the centre circle) moves one space anti-clockwise, as the sequence progresses.

Rule 3 = the outer circles move one space clockwise, as the sequence progresses.

Figure B can be ruled out because the black dot at the bottom centre, should be white, and the black circle should be one space anti-clockwise. Figure C can be ruled out because there should be a black circle at the top centre (outer edge). Figure D can be ruled out because this is an exact replica of figure 3. Figure E can be ruled out because the centred circle should be black, not white.

Q5. A

Rule 1 = the number of points of the large shape should match the number of points on the black star-shape.

Figure A is the odd one out because the large shape contains three points, whereas the number of points on the star-shape is five; therefore this makes it the odd one out.

Q6. B

Rule 1 = the shapes opposite each other should be of the same pattern.

Figure B is the odd one out because the pattern in the square (and opposite the black circle) are not of the same colour and pattern. Either the circle should be changed to the same diagonal black and white lines, or the square should be changed to black.

Q7. C

Rule 1 = all the sides of all the shapes in the figure, should add up to twelve.

Figure C is the odd one out because the sides of the shapes only add up to eleven; therefore this makes Figure C the odd one out.

Q8. D

Rule 1 = box 1 and 3 are horizontal reflections of each other.

Rule 2 = box 2 and 4 are vertical reflections of each other.

Rule 3 = the sequence follows the pattern of: horizontal reflection, vertical reflection, horizontal reflection, vertical etc.

Figure A can be ruled out because this is a reflection of box 4. Figure B can be ruled out because the dashed line should be the other side of the incomplete square; the reflection line should be where the line is missing from the square. Figure C can be ruled out because this is a reflection of box 5. Figure E can be ruled out because this is a reflection of box 2.

Q9. C

Rule 1 = the shape needs to contain a line symmetry.

Figure A can be ruled out because the shape does not contain a line of symmetry. Figure B can be ruled out because the shape does not contain a line of symmetry. Figure D can be ruled out because the shape does not contain a line of symmetry. Figure E can be ruled out because she shape does not contain a line of symmetry.

Q10. C

Rule 1 = the large shape contains a smaller version of itself.

Figure A can be ruled out because the large trapezoid shape is not the same as the small triangle shape. Figure B can be ruled out because the large pentagon shape is not the same as the small circle shape. Figure D can be ruled out because the large 'pie' shape is not the same as the small moon shape. Figure E can be ruled out because the large diamond shape is not the same as the small square shape.

Q11. D

Rule 1 = the right side of the hourglass shape should contain a black triangle.

Figure D is the odd one out because this is the only figure that does not contain a black triangle on the right side of the hourglass shape; therefore this makes the figure the odd one out.

Q12. B

Rule 1 = the number of lines inside the shape has to be one line less than the number of sides of the large shape. For example, a triangle has three sides, therefore it will contain two lines.

Figure A can be ruled out because the number of lines inside the hexagon should be five, not four. Figure C can be ruled out because the number of lines inside the pentagon should be four, not five. Figure D can be ruled out because the number of lines inside the square should be three, not four. Figure E can be ruled out because the number of lines inside the trapezoid should be three, not two.

Q13. B

Rule 1 = the line rotates 45° clockwise as the sequence progresses.

Rule 2 = the line alternates between being in the foreground and being in the background.

Rule 3 = the shapes follow the pattern of 2D shapes then 3D shapes, 2D shapes then 3D shapes and so forth. It alternates between squares (and cubes) and circles (and cylinders).

Figure A can be ruled out because the cube needs to be in the foreground, not in the background. Figure C can be ruled out because the shape in the centre needs to be a cube, not a circle; also the line needs to be vertical, not horizontal. Figure D can be ruled out because the shape in the centre needs to be a cube, not a circle; also the line needs to be vertical, not diagonal. Figure E can be ruled out because there needs to be a vertical line in the background (behind the cube).

Q14. E

Rule 1 = the arrows move one point anti-clockwise as the sequence progresses.

Rule 2 = the arrows point to where the next shape should be positioned.

Rule 3 = the number of arrows determine how many sides the next shape should contain.

Rule 4 = the shapes alternate from white to black.

Figure A can be ruled out because a black triangle should be in the position of the white square. Figure B can be ruled out because the black triangle should be in the top right corner; and the arrows should be in the bottom right corner. Figure C can be ruled out because the triangle should be black not white; and the arrows should be in the bottom right corner, not bottom left. Figure D can be ruled out because the white square should be replaced with a black triangle.

Q15. B

Rule 1 = the shapes alternate between circles and triangles.

Rule 2 = the shapes follow the size pattern of: small, medium, large and repeats.

Rule 3 = the shapes follow the colour pattern of, white, striped, black and repeats.

Figure A can be ruled out because the striped triangle should be black. Figure C can be ruled out because the shape should be a large black triangle, not a medium black circle. Figure D can be ruled out because the shape should be a large black triangle, not a large black circle. Figure E can be ruled out because the shape should be a large black triangle, not a small black triangle.

Q16. C

Rule 1 = all of the stars in the figure must be five-pointed.

Rule 2 = one of the stars must be overlapping a side of the larger shape. Figure A can be ruled out because the stars need to be five-pointed, not four-pointed. Figure B can be ruled out because all the stars need to be five-pointed; one of the stars is only four-pointed. Figure D can be ruled out because none of the stars are overlapping the side of the larger shape. Figure E can be ruled out because the star is a six-pointed star; it needs to be a five- pointed star. Also, the star is not overlapping any of the sides of the larger shape.

Q17. D

Rule 1 = the arrow is being rotated 90° clockwise in the sequence.

Figure D is the odd one out because the arrow has been reflected instead of rotated, therefore makes it the odd one out.

Q18. D

Rule 1 = all of the figures contain the same number of arrows as there are pentagons.

Figure D is the odd one out because all of the other figures contain equal numbers of arrows as there are pentagons. Whereas in Figure D, there is only one arrow but two pentagons; therefore this makes this figure the odd one out.

Q19. C

Rule 1 = the whole figure has been rotated 90° clockwise.

Figure A can be ruled out because this is an exact replica of box 4. Figure B can be ruled out because this is a reflection of box 2. Figure D can be ruled out because both triangles have been rotated; whereas the rest of the figure has been reflected.

Q20. C

Rule 1 = the shapes must contain diagonal lines going from bottom left to top right.

Figure A can be ruled out because the diagonal lines are going from top left to bottom right; they should be going from bottom left to top right. Figure B can be ruled out because the lines are going vertical, they should be going diagonal. Figure D can be ruled out because the lines are going horizontal, and they should be going diagonal.

Q21. A

Rule 1 = in the top left corner, the shapes alternate between circles and squares.

Rule 2 = in the top left corner, the shapes change colour from black to white. Rule 3 = in the top left corner, the shapes increase in size as the sequence progresses.

Rule 4 = in the bottom right corner, the shapes decrease in size as the sequence progresses.

Figure B can be ruled out because the circle in the top left corner needs to be black, not white. Figure C can be ruled out because the square in the bottom right corner needs to be white, not black. Figure D can be ruled out because the circle in the bottom right corner, needs to be a white square; the square in the top left corner needs to be a black circle. Figure E can be ruled out because the circle in the bottom right corner needs to be a white square.

Q22. C

Rule 1 = the black triangle moves one place to the right as the sequence progresses (middle, right, left, middle, right, left and so forth).

Rule 2 = the black cross moves one point anti-clockwise around the four corners of the square.

Figure A can be ruled out because the cross should be in the bottom right corner, not the top right corner. Figure B can be ruled out because the black triangle should be on the middle row, on the right side; the cross should be in the bottom right corner. Figure D can be ruled out because the black triangle should be on the middle row, on the right side. Figure E can be ruled out because the black triangle should be on the middle row, on the right side, not in the centre.

Q23. C

Rule 1 = working in a clockwise manner, the sequence should follow: square, triangle, circle; and then repeat.

Figure C is the odd one out because the sequence pattern is different from the other figures. Instead of following the pattern: square, triangle circle; it follows the pattern of square, circle, triangle.

Q24. E

Rule 1 = the pattern follows nine different shapes, and then the sequence is repeated.

Figure A can be ruled out because this would need to be flipped vertically in order for the squares to be in the correct position. Figure

B can be ruled out because the squares need to be rotated 90° anti-clockwise. Figure C can be ruled out because the squares need to be rotated 90° clockwise. Figure D can be ruled out because the next shape in the sequence would be two squares, not a triangle.

Q25. D

Rule 1 = the square moves three places clockwise around the edge of the square, as the sequence progresses.

Rule 2 = the colour pattern alternates between: black, grey and white and repeats.

Figure A can be ruled out because the grey square should be on the middle row on the left side of the square. Figure B can be ruled out because the white square should be a grey square. Figure C can be ruled out because the black square in the top left corner should be moved one place down (so it is on the middle row). Figure E can be ruled out because the black square in the middle of the first row, should be a grey square on the middle row, on the left side of the square.

Q26. B

Rule 1 = starting from the end of the patterned squares (bottom left corner), the sequence follows the pattern of: removing two shaded squares from the end of the sequence.

Figure A can be ruled out because there should be two squares left, not three. Figure C can be ruled out because the grey square should remain a black square. Figure D can be ruled out because the two squares that have been removed should be the squares that remain; two black squares should remain on the first row, in the third and fourth squares.

Q27. C

Rule 1 = starting from the white dot in the bottom left corner, it moves two places clockwise, around the edge of the figure.

Rule 2 = starting from the white dot second on the first row, it moves three places clockwise, around the edge of the figure.

Figure A can be ruled out because the white dot third on the first row should be the second dot on the first row. Figure B can be ruled out because the white dot in the bottom right corner should be one place above it; the white dot on the first row should also be moved one place anti-clockwise. Figure D can be ruled out because the white dot on the third row should be the second dot on the first row. Also, the white dot on the second row should be moved one place clockwise.

Q28. E

Rule 1 = the black circle follows the pattern of: centre, left, centre, top, centre, right and so forth.

Rule 2 = the cross switches from a cross sign to a plus sign as the sequence progresses.

Rule 3 = the cross/plus signs move around the figure one point anti-clockwise, as the sequence progresses.

Figure A can be ruled out because the plus sign should be a cross sign. Figure B can be ruled out because the black dot should be in the centre of the figure; the plus sign should be a cross sign and should be placed in the bottom left corner. Figure C can be ruled out because the black dot should be in the centre of the figure; the cross should be positioned in the bottom left corner. Figure D can be ruled out because the cross should be positioned in the bottom left corner.

Q29. B

Rule 1 = the shape with the most number of sides should have a solid outline.

Rule 2 = the shape with the least number of sides should have a dotted outline.

Rule 3 = the shape with the middle number of sides should have a dashed outline.

Figure A can be ruled out because the pentagon should have a dashed outline and the diamond should have a dotted outline. Figure C can be ruled out because the pentagon should not have a solid outline, it should have a dashed outline. Figure D can be ruled out because the arrow should not have a dotted outline, it should have a solid outline. Also, the pentagon should not have a solid outline, it should have a dashed outline. Figure E can be ruled out because the arrow should have a solid outline, and the diamond should have a dotted outline.

Q30. A

Rule 1 = starting from the middle four squares, the arrow and the moon shapes move around the centred squares one place anti-clockwise.

Rule 2 = the heart shape moves two places clockwise, around the outer edge, as the sequence progresses.

Rule 3 = the star moves three places clockwise, around the outer edge, as the sequence progresses.

Figure B can be ruled out because the star should be positioned one space above where it is; it should be in the last box on the third row. Figure C can be ruled out because all the shapes need to move down one row. Figure D can be ruled out because the moon and arrow shapes are in the wrong positions; the moon shape should be where the arrow shape is; and the arrow shape should be where the moon shape is.

Q31. C

Rule 1 = a black shape should remain at the top of the figure.

Figure C is the odd one out because all of the other figures contain a black shape at the top of the figure; whereas Figure C contains a black shape at the bottom of the sequence and therefore makes it the odd one out.

Q32. D

Rule 1 = a grey shape must be at the front of the figure.

Rule 2 = the shapes in each figure must be the same.

Figure A can be ruled out because the shape at the front is black; it should be grey. Figure B can be ruled out because the shape at the front is black; it should be grey. Figure C can be ruled out because the shape at the front is white; it should be grey. Figure E can be ruled out because the shape at the front is black; it should be grey. Also, the shapes in the figure need to be the same, so the shapes should all be trapezoids, or they should all be diamonds.

Q33. D

Rule 1 = you need to fold along the creases of the cube, so that the shapes are on the outside of the cube.

Figure A can be ruled out because the lines on the side would need to be horizontal, not vertical. Figure B can be ruled out because the lines on the top would need to be vertical not horizontal. Figure C can be ruled out because the star is unable to be on the right side of the vertical lines.

Q34. E

Rule 1 = the small shape must be the same as the large shape.

Rule 2 = the small shape must be interlinked on the left side of the large shape. Figure E is the odd one out because all of the other figures contain a small shape that is interlinked with the large shape on the left side; whereas Figure E interlinks the smaller shape on the right side of the larger shape; and therefore makes it the odd one out.

Q35. B

As the series goes on, a smaller circle appears in the middle of the existing circle with the opposite shading.

As well as this, the small circle on in the corner moves around the square clockwise once each time. It also changes shading each time it moves a place.

Therefore, shape b) is the correct answer. The circle in the middle of the larger shape is black and the smaller circle on the corner moves clockwise one place and changes to white.

Q36. E

Rule 1 = the pattern in the small shape should be diagonal (from top left to bottom right).

Figure E is the odd one out because all of the other figures contain diagonal lines going from top left to bottom right; whereas Figure E contains a diagonal pattern going from bottom left to top right and therefore makes it the odd one out.

Q37. A

A is a rotation of the shape on the left. In b), c) and d), some of the shading on the small shapes and the direction of the arrows have changed.

In b), one of the arrows of equal length is facing the wrong way. In c), the central oval is shaded when it should be white. In d), the rectangle is unshaded when it should be shaded. A) is the only shape which is a direct rotation of the example shape.

Q38. C

Rule 1 = the centred circles contain a dotted circle that rotates one place clockwise as the sequence progresses.

Rule 2 = the diagonal line going from bottom left to top right moves two places anti-clockwise, around the outer edge of the sequence.

Rule 3 = the diagonal line going from top left to bottom right moves three places clockwise, around the outer edge of the sequence.

Rule 4 = if the diagonal lines coincide with one another, that dot becomes patterned with both diagonal line types running through the shape.

Figures A, B and D can all be ruled out because the patterned dots are not in the correct position.

Q39. A

Rule 1 = the shapes must be able to make up a square.

Figure B can be ruled out because these three shapes will not make up a square. Figure C can be ruled out because these two shapes will not make up a square. Figure D can be ruled out because these two circles cannot make up a square. Figure E can be ruled out because these three shapes will not make up a square.

Q40. C

Rule 1 = the shape on top is a reflection of the shape on the bottom.

Rule 2 = one half of the figure is black and the other half is white.

Rule 3 = the shapes must join at a point.

Figure C is the odd one out because all of the other figures show reflections of the shapes; whereas Figure C contains a four-pointed star and a five-pointed star, and so this does not mirror the same shape and therefore is the odd one out.

INDUCTIVE REASONING
SECTION 6

QUESTION 1

Fill in the gap in order to complete the sequence.

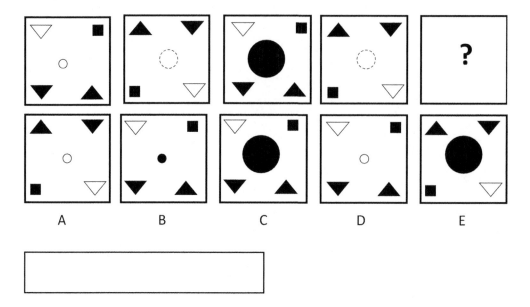

QUESTION 2

Fill in the gap in order to complete the sequence.

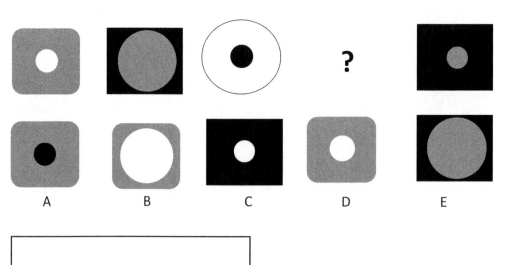

QUESTION 3

What comes next in the sequence?

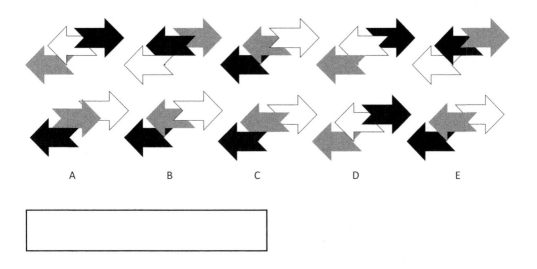

| A | B | C | D | E |

QUESTION 4

Which figure is the odd one out?

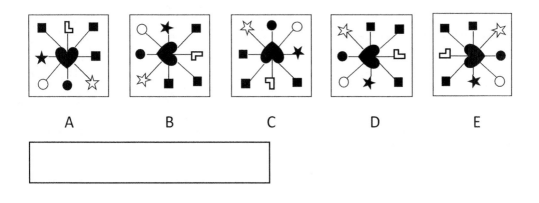

| A | B | C | D | E |

QUESTION 5

Complete the pair using the first pair to help you.

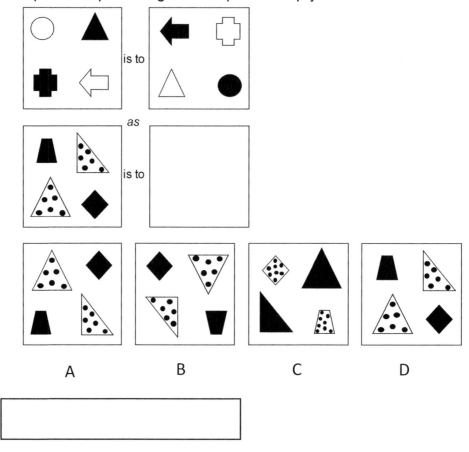

A   B   C   D

QUESTION 6

Which answer shape is a rotation of the example shape?

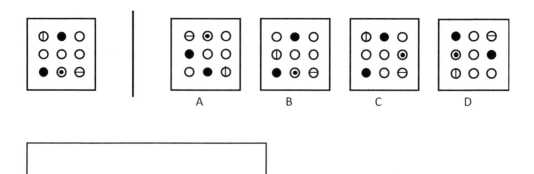

A   B   C   D

QUESTION 7

Fill in the gap in order to complete the sequence.

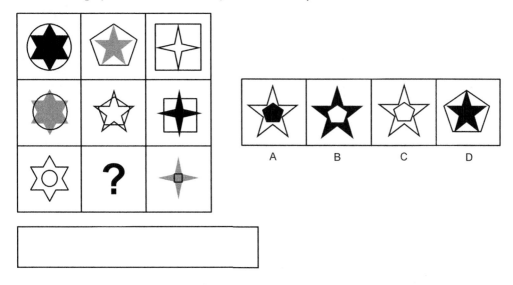

QUESTION 8

Fill in the gap in order to complete the sequence.

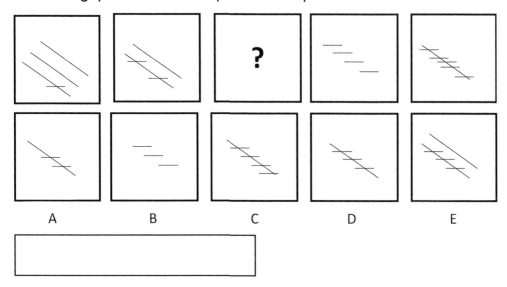

QUESTION 9

Fill in the gap in order to complete the sequence.

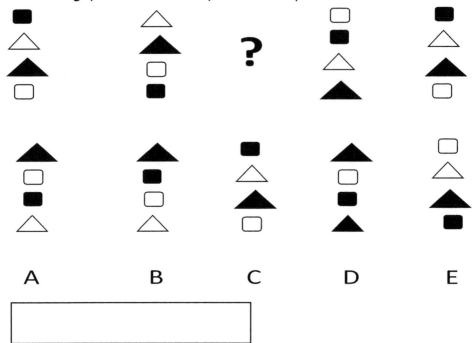

QUESTION 10

What comes next in the sequence?

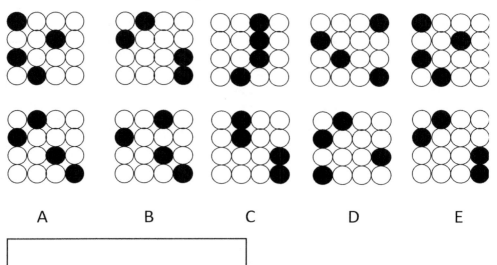

QUESTION 11

The middle row of boxes create a rule that has been applied to the boxes directly above them. Which answer option (A to E) corresponds to the rule under the box with the question mark?

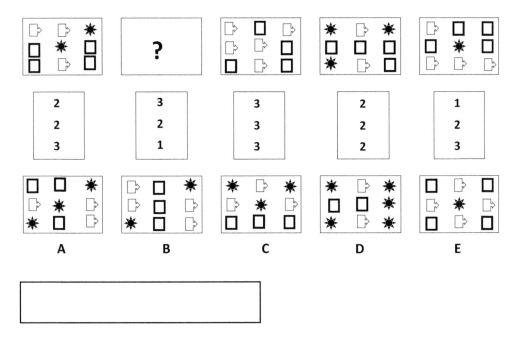

QUESTION 12

Which figure is the odd one out?

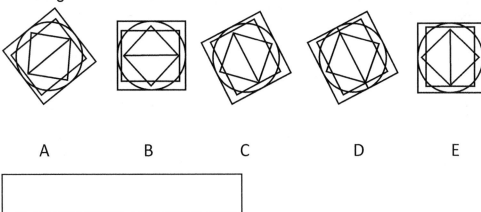

QUESTION 13

Find the odd one out from the four shapes below.

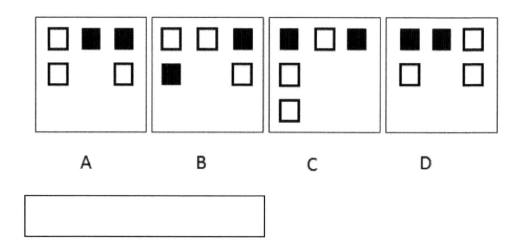

A   B   C   D

QUESTION 14

Fill in the gap in order to complete the sequence.

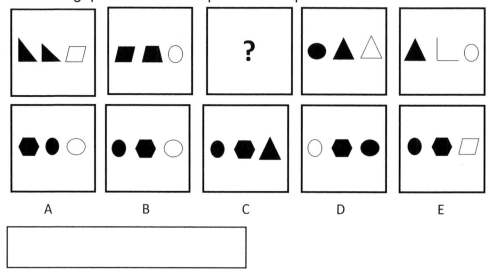

A   B   C   D   E

QUESTION 15

Which figure is the odd one out?

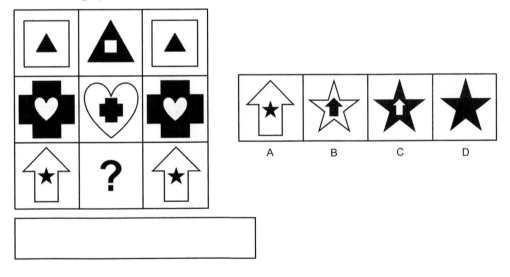

A   B   C   D   E

QUESTION 16

Fill in the gap in order to complete the sequence.

QUESTION 17

Fill in the gap in order to complete the sequence.

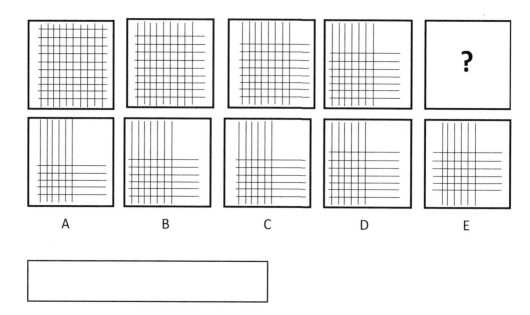

QUESTION 18

Fill in the gap in order to complete the sequence.

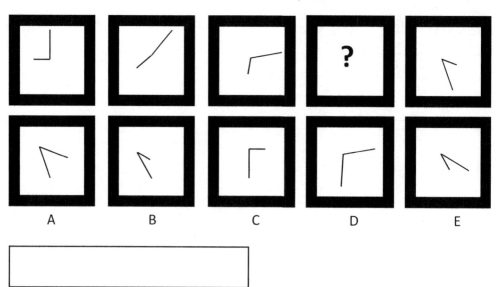

QUESTION 19

Fill in the gap in order to complete the sequence.

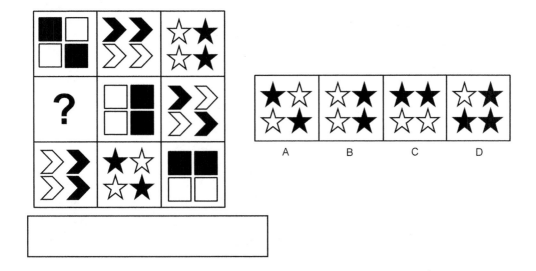

QUESTION 20

Fill in the gap in order to complete the sequence.

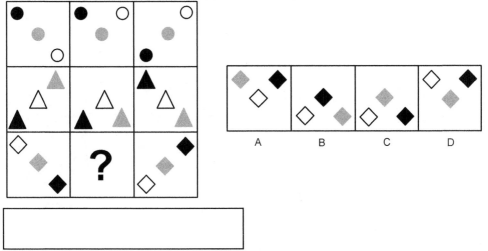

QUESTION 21

Which Answer Figure fits in with the two Question Figures?

Question Figures

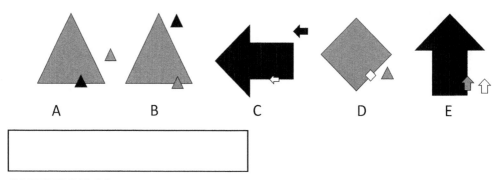

Answer Figures

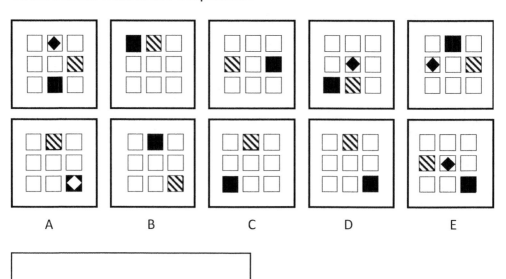

| A | B | C | D | E |

QUESTION 22

What comes next in the sequence?

| A | B | C | D | E |

QUESTION 23

Which Answer Figure fits in with the two Question Figures?

Question Figures

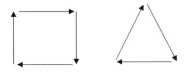

Answer Figures

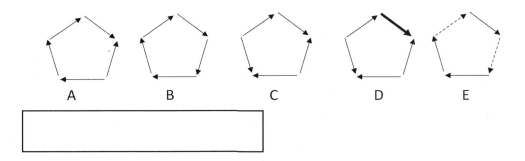

| A | B | C | D | E |

QUESTION 24

Which figure is the odd one out?

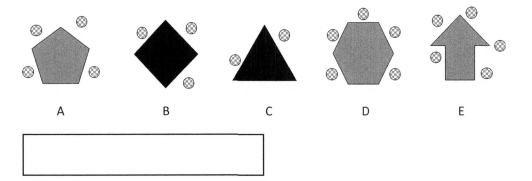

| A | B | C | D | E |

QUESTION 25

Fill in the gap in order to complete the sequence.

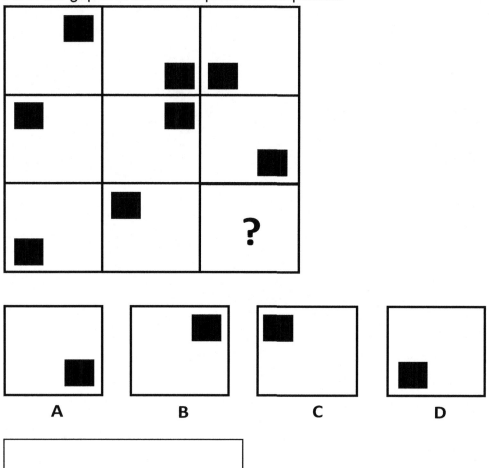

A   B   C   D

QUESTION 26

Fill in the gap in order to complete the sequence.

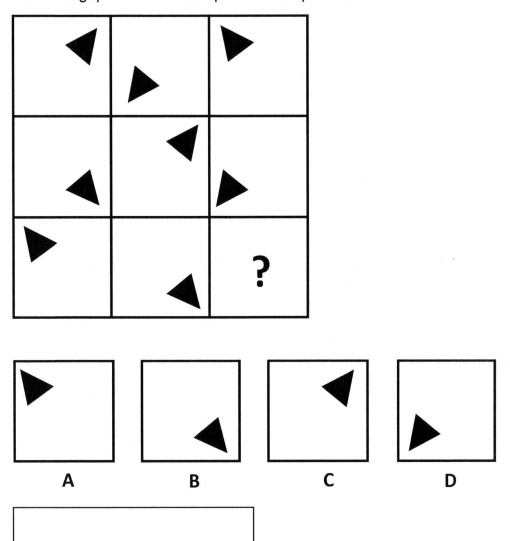

A   B   C   D

QUESTION 27

Which Answer Figure fits in with the two Question Figures?

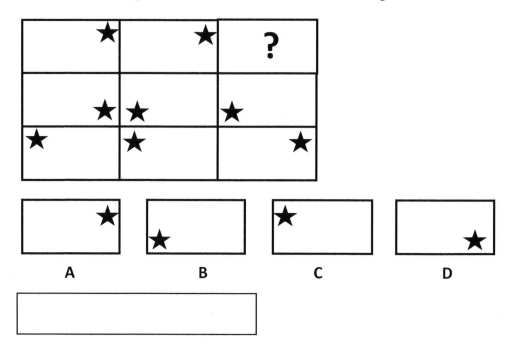

A   B   C   D

QUESTION 28

Work out which of the cubes can be made from the cube net.

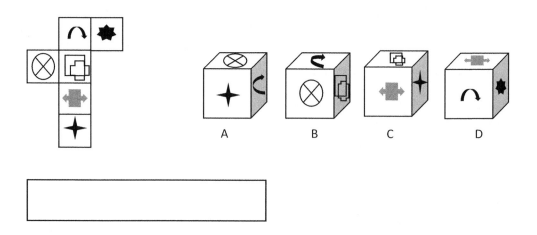

A   B   C   D

QUESTION 29

Which figure is the odd one out?

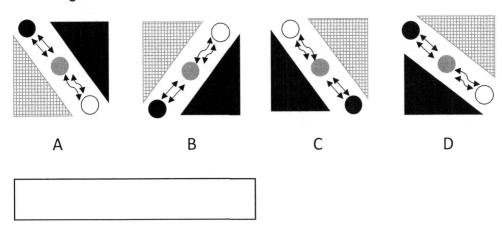

| A | B | C | D |

QUESTION 30

Which figure is the odd one out?

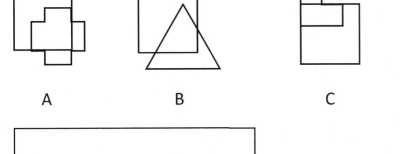
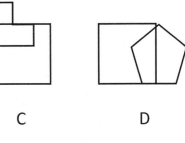

| A | B | C | D |

QUESTION 31

Fill in the gap in order to complete the sequence.

125	216	343	?

729	512	457	686
A	B	C	D

QUESTION 32

Fill in the gap in order to complete the sequence.

23	29	?	37

31	32	40	41
A	B	C	D

QUESTION 33

Which Answer Figure fits in with the two Question Figures?

Question Figures

Answer Figures

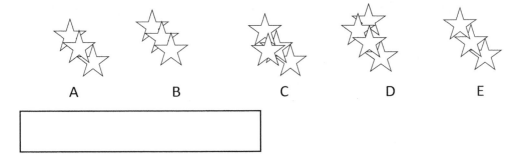

QUESTION 34

Which figure is the odd one out?

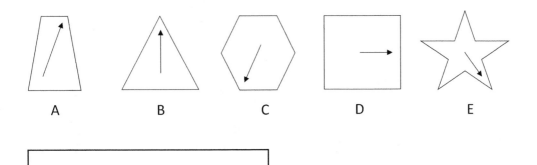

QUESTION 35

What comes next in the sequence?

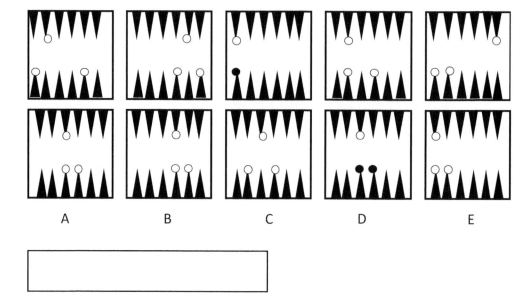

 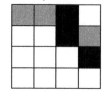 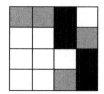

A   B   C   D   E

QUESTION 36

Fill in the gap in order to complete the sequence.

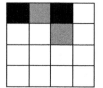 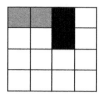 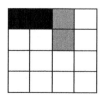 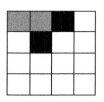

A   B   C   D

QUESTION 37

What comes next in the sequence?

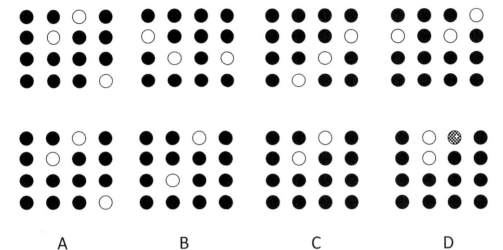

A   B   C   D

QUESTION 38

Which figure is the odd one out?

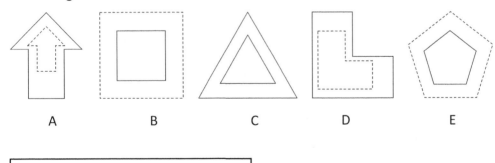

A   B   C   D   E

QUESTION 39

Work out which of the cubes can be made from the cube net.

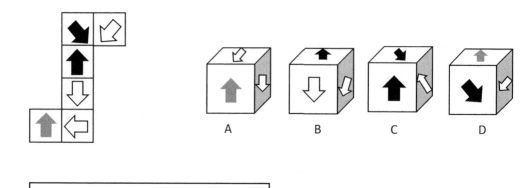

A	B	C	D

QUESTION 40

Which Answer Figure fits in with the three Question Figures?

Question Figures

Answer Figures

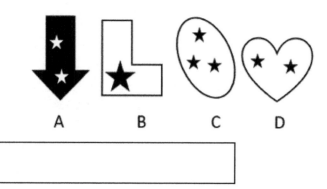

A	B	C	D

ANSWERS TO SECTION 6

Q1. D

Rule 1 = the circle in the centre follows the pattern of: white, patterned, black, patterned, white and repeats.

Rule 2 = the circle also increases in size from small, medium to large and repeats.

Rule 3 = the two shapes diagonal from one another switch place in every even box. It alternates between these two forms.

Figure A can be ruled out because the shapes in the corners of the square need to switch positions with the shape diagonal to it. Figure B can be ruled out because the circle in the centre of the figure should be white, not black. Figure C can be ruled out because the circle in the centre of the figure should be a small white circle, not a large black circle. Figure E can be ruled out because the circle in the centre of the figure should be a small white circle, not a large black circle. Also, the shapes in the corner of the square need to switch positions with the shape diagonal to it.

Q2. B

Rule 1 = the large shape alternates between a square with rounded edges, a square and a circle.

Rule 2 = the large shape changes colour from grey, to black, to white and repeats.

Rule 3 = the shape inside the larger shape alternates from small to big.

Rule 4 = the colour pattern of the inner shapes alternate from white, to grey, to black and repeats.

Figure A can be ruled out because the circle inside the larger shape needs to be a large white circle, not a small black circle. Figure C can be ruled out because the large shape needs to be a grey square with rounded edges. Also, the inner shape needs to be a large white circle, not a small white circle. Figure D can be ruled out because the inner circle needs to be a large white circle, not a small white circle. Figure E can be ruled out because the large square needs to be grey and have rounded edges. Also, the inner shape needs to be a large white circle, not a large grey circle.

Q3. C

Rule 1 = the colour sequence moves down one space as the sequence progresses.

Rule 2 = the top and the bottom shape alternate being in the foreground and being in the background.

Figure A can be ruled out because the middle arrow is pointing in the wrong direction. Figure B can be ruled out because the white arrow should be in the background, and the black arrow should be in the foreground. Figure D can be ruled out because the colour pattern should be: white, grey, black; not black, white and grey. Also, the top arrow should be in the background, and the bottom arrow should be in the foreground. Figure E can be ruled out because the grey arrow should not be in the foreground; the white arrow should be in the background, and the black arrow should be in the foreground.

Q4. D

Rule 1 = each figure is being rotated.

Figure D is the odd one out because all of the other figures are being rotated, whereas Figure D has been reflected after it has been rotated and therefore makes it the odd one out.

Q5. C

The first pair sees two black shapes switch places and become white and the two white shapes switch places and become black.

This method can be applied to the second pair where two black shapes change places and become spotted and the two spotted shapes switch places and become black.

Q6. D

D) is a rotation of the shape on the left. In a), b) and c), some of the small circles within the square have switched places and therefore they cannot be rotations of the example shape.

In a), one of the black dots is in the wrong place, in b), one of the lined dots is in the wrong place and in c) one of the dots with a dot in the centre is wrong. D) is the only shape which is a rotation of the example shape.

Q7. B

Rule 1 = the sequence follows: from box 1 to 3, a six sided star, a five sided star and a four sided star. These stars are placed inside a shape.

Rule 2 = The next row has the same star shapes, but is placed half in – half out of another shape. The colour sequence moves along one space each time.

Rule 3 = the last row, has the star shapes outside the other shape. The colour pattern has also moved one space again.

Figure A, C and D can all be ruled out because none of these figures contain a white pentagon shape inside a black five-pointed star.

Q8. D

Rule 1 = the number of diagonal lines decrease by one, once it reaches zero, then the lines increase by one.

Rule 2 = the horizontal line is added by one each time to the same diagonal line.

Figure A can be ruled out because there should be three horizontal lines, not two. Figure B can be ruled out because there should be a diagonal line running through all of the horizontal lines. Figure C can be ruled out because there should be three horizontal lines, not four. Figure E can be ruled out because there should only be one diagonal line, not two; the diagonal line that remains should be the one running through the horizontal lines.

Q9. A

Rule 1 = the shapes in the vertical line move down three spaces as the sequence progresses.

Rule 2 = once the shape reaches the bottom, it starts back at the beginning of the vertical line.

Figure B can be ruled out because the two squares should follow the colour pattern: white then black, not black then white. Figure C can be ruled out because this is an exact replica of the first vertical line in the sequence. Figure D can be ruled out because both triangles cannot be black; the last triangle should be white, not black. Figure E can be ruled out because the triangles should be the first and last in the vertical line, not in the middle.

Q10. E

Rule 1 = on the first row, the black dot moves one space, left to right.

Rule 2 = on the second row, the black dot moves two spaces, left to right.

Rule 3 = on the third row, the black dot moves three spaces, left to right.

Rule 4 = on the fourth row, the black dot moves two spaces, left to right.

Figure A can be ruled out because the black dot on the third row should be the last dot on that row. Figure B can be ruled out because the black dot on the first row should be the second dot, not the third dot. Also, the black dot on the third row should be the last dot on that row. Figure C can be ruled out because the black dot on the second row should be the first dot, not the second. Figure D can be ruled out because the black dot on the last row should be the last dot, not the first dot.

Q11. E

The rule in this question sees the number '2' dictating the number of sun shapes in the pattern above. The rule being applied to box with the question mark means that one sun shape should appear in the answer.

Q12. D

Figure D is the odd one out because all of the other figures are rotations of one another; whereas Figure D has been manipulated; the horizontal line inside the diamond shape has been stretched out and reaches the edge of the square (it should only reach the edge of the diamond shape).

Q13. C

All of the 4 shapes have the same amount of small squares, with two black and three white. However, c) is the only one with a square at the bottom.

Q14. B

Rule 1 = the first shape in each figure is the last shape of the previous figure.

Rule 2 = the colour pattern always follows: black, black and white.

Rule 3 = the number of sides of the shapes altogether decreases by one as the sequence progresses.

Q15. D

Rule 1 = the shape with the fewest number of sides should be white.

Figure D is the odd one out because all of the other figures contain two shapes; the one with the fewest number of sides is white, and the one with the most number of sides contains a diagonal pattern; whereas Figure D has diagonal lines running through the shape with the fewest number of sides (which should be white).

Q16. C

Rule 1 = in each row, it contains a large shape and a small shape; the small shape becomes the large shape and the large shape becomes the small shape in the next box.

Figure A can be ruled out because this is an exact replica of the first and third figures in the third row. Figure B can be ruled out because the black star should remain black, and the white arrow should remain white (the colour pattern for each shape stays the same throughout each row). Figure D can be ruled out because the black star needs to contain a white arrow inside the shape.

Q17. C

Rule 1 = one line from the top of the horizontal lines is removed as the sequence progresses.

Rule 2 = one line from the far right side of the vertical lines is removed as the sequence progresses.

Figure A can be ruled out because there should be six horizontal lines, not five. Figure B can be ruled out because there should be six vertical lines, not seven. Figure D can be ruled out because there should be six horizontal lines, not seven. Figure E can be ruled out because the lines have been removed from the wrong sides; the horizontal line should be removed from the top, not the bottom; and the vertical line should be removed from the far right side, not the left side.

Q18. E

Rule 1 = the big line moves 40°clockwise as the sequence progresses.

Rule 2 = the small line moves 40° anti-clockwise as the sequence progresses.

Figure A can be ruled out because only one line should be big, the other line should be shorter. Figure B can be ruled out because the short line should be a big line; and the big line should be the short line. Figure C can be ruled out because this is a rotation of the first figure in the sequence. Figure D can be ruled out because neither line is in the correct position.

Q19. C

Rule 1 = the shapes move throughout the sequence one space each time. For example, the squares in the first box, on the first row, will be in the second box in the second row, and the third box in the third row.

Rule 2 = the colour pattern moves one space throughout each row.

Figure A can be ruled out because the stars on the top row should be black, and the stars on the bottom should be white. Figure B can be ruled out because the stars on the top row should be black, not white and black; and the stars on the bottom row should be white, not white and black. Figure D can be ruled out because the stars on the bottom should both be white, not black and white.

Q20. D

Rule 1 = from box 1 to box 2, the shape at the bottom of the diagonal line moves to the top right corner.

Rule 2 = from box 2 to box 3, the shape at the top left corner will move down to the bottom left corner.

Figure A can be ruled out because the white diamond and the grey diamond should be in each other's positions. Figure B can be ruled out because the diamonds should be in the top half of the square, not in the bottom half. Also, the colour pattern of the diamonds is incorrect, from left to right it should be white, grey and black. Figure C can be ruled out because this is a reflection of what the answer should look like.

Q21. C

Rule 1 = the large shape is the same shape as the other two smaller shapes.

Rule 2 = the shape interlinked with the larger shape on the right side should be white.

Rule 3 = the colour outside the larger shape should be the same as the larger shape.

Figure A can be ruled out because the triangle interlinked with the large triangle should be white, not black. Figure B can be ruled out because the triangle interlinked with the large triangle should be white, not grey. Also, the triangle on the outside should be the same colour as the large triangle (grey); as opposed to being a different colour (black). Figure D can be ruled out because the small triangle on the outside of the diamond should be the same shape as the diamond, not a triangle. Figure E can be ruled out because the arrow interlinked with the large arrow should be white, not grey. Also, the arrow on the outside should be the same colour as the large arrow (black) as opposed to being a different colour (white).

Q22. D

Rule 1 = the diamond moves one place from right to left, once it reaches the end of the row, it begins on the right side of the next row.

Rule 2 = the black square moves three spaces around the outer edge in a clockwise motion.

Rule 3 = the diagonal patterned square moves two spaces around the outer edge in an anti-clockwise motion.

Rule 4 = if a diamond and a patterned or black square coincide, the diamond disappears behind the square.

Figure A can be ruled out because the diamond should disappear behind the black square, not become white. Figure B can be ruled out because the black square should be where the patterned square goes; and the patterned square should be where the black square is. Figure C can be ruled out because the black square should be in the bottom right corner, not bottom left. Figure E can be ruled out because the diamond should have disappeared behind the black square; and the patterned square should be the middle square on the first row.

Q23. B

Rule 1 = the arrows make up a shape.

Rule 2 = the arrows must follow a clockwise direction.

Figure A can be ruled out because the two arrows on the right side of the pentagon are pointing towards each other; they should both be pointing in a clockwise direction. Figure C can be ruled out because two arrows are in the incorrect position. The arrow bottom right of the pentagon should be facing downwards, to start the next arrow; and the arrow bottom left of the pentagon should be facing upwards. Figure D can be ruled out because this is an exact replica of answer option C; the only difference is that there is a bold arrow line, which there shouldn't be. Figure E can be ruled out because two of the arrow lines are patterned; they should all be the same pattern throughout (in this case, solid lines).

Q24. E

Rule 1 = the number of dots should be one less than the number of sides of the shape.

Figure E is the odd one out. This is because all of the other figures contain a number of dots equivalent to one less than the number of sides of the larger shape. In Figure E, there are seven sides to the shape, therefore there should be six dots; however there are only five dots.

Q25. B

Rule 1 = the square moves around one point of the larger square in a clockwise manner and follows on through each row.

Figure A can be ruled out because the black square should be in the top right corner, not the bottom right corner. Figure C can be ruled out because the black square should be in the top right corner, not the top left corner. Figure D can be ruled out because the square should be in the top right corner, not the bottom left corner.

Q26. C

Rule 1 = the triangles point faces the corner of the square.

Rule 2 = the triangles follow the pattern of: top right, bottom left, top left, bottom right and repeats.

Figure A can be ruled out because the triangle should be in the top right corner, not the top left. Figure B can be ruled out because the triangle should be in the top right corner, not the bottom right. Figure D can be ruled out because the triangle should be in the top right corner, not the bottom left.

Q27. D

Rule 1 = the star remains in the same place for every two boxes.

Rule 2 = after every two boxes, the star moves one point clockwise around the rectangles corner.

Figure A can be ruled out because the star should be in the bottom right corner, not the top right. Figure B can be ruled out because the star should be in the bottom right corner, not the bottom left. Figure C can be ruled out because the star should be in the bottom right corner, not the top left.

Q28. B

Rule 1 = you need to fold along the creases of the cube, so that the shapes are on the outside of the cube.

Figure A can be ruled out because the black arrow would need to be replaced with the grey square with the two arrows. Figure C can be ruled out because the diamond shape would need to be replaced with the black star. Figure D can be ruled out because the grey square with the arrows would need to be replaced with the black diamond.

Q29. D

Rule 1 = the figures should all be reflections of one another.

Figure D is the odd one out because all of the other figures are reflections of one another; whereas Figure D is a reflection and a rotation.

Q30. A

Rule 1 = the shapes interlinked must create an inner shape that contains four sides.

Figure A is the odd one out because all of the other figures create an inner shape which contains four sides; whereas Figure A creates an inner shape that has six sides and therefore makes it the odd one out.

Q31. B

Rule 1 = the sequence are cube numbers, starting from 5^3 (5 x 5 x 5).

Figure A can be ruled out because the next number in the sequence needs to be 8^3 (8 x 8 x 8), which equals 512, not 729 (729 is the cubed number for 9). Figure C can be ruled out because 457 is not a cubed number. Figure D can be ruled out because 686 is just double the previous number, it is not a cubed number.

Q32. A

Rule 1 = the sequence are prime numbers in order. (A prime number is a number that only multiplies by 1 and itself).

Figure B can be ruled out because 32 is not a prime number; the numbers 1, 2, 4, 8 16 and 32 all go into 32. Figure C can be ruled out because 40 is not a prime number; the numbers 1, 2, 4, 5, 8, 10, 20 and 40 all go into 40. Figure D can be ruled out because, and although 41 is a prime number, it does not fit in the third box within the sequence.

Q33. E

Rule 1 = the top shape must be at the foreground.

Figure A can be ruled out because the top star should be the star in the foreground, not the middle star. Figure B can be ruled out because the top star should be at the forefront, not the bottom star. Figure C can be ruled out because the top star needs to be in the foreground of the figure, and instead the middle star is at the front. Figure D can be ruled out because the top star should be the star at the front, not the second star from the bottom.

Q34. D

Rule 1 = the arrow must point towards a corner of the shape.

Figure D is the odd one out because all of the other figures contain an arrow pointing towards a corner of the large shape, whereas in Figure D, the arrow is pointing to a side, not a corner and therefore makes it the odd one out.

Q35. A

Rule 1 = the dot on the top row follows the sequence of moving from left to right in the pattern of: moving three spaces, two spaces, 1 space, 4 spaces, 3 spaces and so forth.

Rule 2 = the first dot on the bottom row moves three spaces backwards.

Rule 3 = the second dot on the bottom row moves one space forwards.

Rule 4 = if any of the dots coincide with one another, it becomes a black dot.

Figure B can be ruled out because all the dots need to move back one space. Figure C can be ruled out because the first dot on the bottom row should be moved one space forwards. Figure D can be ruled out because the dots on the bottom row should be white, not black. Figure E can be ruled out because all the dots should be moved forwards two spaces.

Q36. B

Rule 1 = the sequence adds two coloured boxes each time.

Figure A can be ruled out because the sequence begins with two grey squares in the first and second box, these cannot change colour. Figure C can be ruled out because the first two boxes should be grey, and the next two boxes should be black. Figure D can be ruled out because the black square on the second row should be moved over one space.

Q37. C

Rule 1 = the white circle in the inner four circles rotates one place anti-clockwise as the sequence progresses.

Rule 2 = starting with the white circle on the first row, it moves three places around the outer edge anti-clockwise.

Rule 3 = starting with the white circle on the bottom row, it moves one space around the outer edge anti-clockwise.

Figure A can be ruled out because the white circle in the bottom right corner, should be black. Figure B can be ruled out because the white circle in the inner section should be one space above the position it is in. Figure D can be ruled out because the white circle on the top row, should be black.

Q38. C

Rule 1 = the inner shape of the figure must be the same as the larger shape of the figure.

Rule 2 = one shape must be a solid line, and the other shape must be a dashed line.

Figure C is the odd one out because all of the other figures contain one shape with a solid line, and one shape with a dashed line; whereas in Figure C, the two shapes are both solid lines, one line should be dashed and therefore makes it the odd one out.

Q39. C

Rule 1 = you need to fold along the creases of the cube, so that the shapes are on the outside of the cube.

Figure A can be ruled out because the arrow on the side would have to be pointing towards the left. Figure B can be ruled out because the arrow on the right would need to be pointing towards the top left corner. Figure D can be ruled out because the top of the box would need to have a white arrow pointing towards the left side.

Q40. D

Rule 1 = the figure needs to be white and contain two black stars.

Figure A can be ruled out because the large shape needs to be white, not black; and the two white stars need to be black. Figure B can be ruled out because the shape needs to contain two black stars, not one black star. Figure C can be ruled out because the shape needs to contain two black stars, not three.

A FEW FINAL WORDS

You have now reached the end of your Inductive Reasoning testing guide. Hopefully you now feel more comfortable and confident with these tests and will be able to successfully pass any Inductive Reasoning test.

For any psychometric test, there are a few things to remember to help you perform at your best…

REMEMBER – The THREE P's!

I. Prepare.

This may seem relatively obvious, but you will be surprised by how many people fail psychometric testing because they lacked knowledge and understanding of what to expect. Be sure to practice these tests before having to sit a real test. Not only will you become familiar with the testing questions, it will also remove some of the pressure leading up to that all important test. Like anything, the more you practice, the more likely you are to succeed!

2.Perseverance.

You are far more likely to succeed at something if you continuously set out to achieve it. Everybody will experience times when they get setbacks, or obstacles in the way of their goals. The important thing to remember when this happens, is to use those setbacks and obstacles as a way of progressing. It is what you do with your past experiences that helps to determine your success in the future. If you fail at something, consider 'why' you have failed. This will allow you to improve and enhance your performance for next time.

3. Performance.
Performance is a great word. Your performance will determine whether or not you are likely to succeed. Attributes that are often associated with performance are self-belief, motivation and commitment. Self-belief is important for anything you do in your life. It allows you to recognise your own abilities and skills and believe that you can do well. Believing that you can do well is half the battle!

Being fully motivated and committed is often difficult for some people, but we can assure you that, nothing is gained without hard work and determination. If you want to succeed, you will need to put in that extra time and hard work!

The majority of candidates who pass the selection process for their chosen career have a number of common attributes. These are as follows:

I. They believe in themselves.

The first factor is self-belief. Regardless of what anyone tells you, you can pass your tests and get the job that you really want. Just like any test, interview or selection process, you have to be prepared to work hard in order to be successful. Make sure you have the self-belief to pass the Inductive Reasoning test with high scores and fill your mind with positive thoughts.

2. They prepare fully.

The second factor is preparation. Those people who achieve in life prepare fully for every eventuality, and that is what you must do when you prepare for your Inductive Reasoning test. Work very hard and especially concentrate on your weak areas.

3. They are self-motivated.

How much do you want this job? Do you want it, or do you really want it? When you apply for any job you should want it more than anything in the world. Your levels of self-motivation will shine through on your application, whilst sitting the test and also during your interview. For the weeks and months leading up to the selection process, be motivated as best you can and always keep your fitness levels up as this will serve to increase your levels of motivation.

Work hard, stay focused and pass any assessment!

Remember, we have also provided you with some additional free online psychometric tests which will help to improve your competence further in this particular testing area. To gain access, simply go to:

www.PsychometricTestsOnline.co.uk

Good luck with your Inductive Reasoning test. We wish you the best of luck with all your future endeavours!

The how2become team

The How2Become Team

Take a look at our other Reasoning guides!

Each guide is packed full of examples and practice questions, to ensure that you make the most out of your revision time and can aim to achieve 100%!

FOR MORE INFORMATION ON OUR TESTING GUIDES, PLEASE CHECK OUT THE FOLLOWING:

WWW.HOW2BECOME.COM

Get Access To
FREE
Reasoning
Test Questions

www.MyPsychometricTests.co.uk

Printed in Great Britain
by Amazon

11225848R00108